Nehemiah Adams

The Power and Office of the Holy Spirit

Nehemiah Adams

The Power and Office of the Holy Spirit

ISBN/EAN: 9783337029494

Printed in Europe, USA, Canada, Australia, Japan

Cover: Foto ©Lupo / pixelio.de

More available books at **www.hansebooks.com**

RESULT OF COUNCIL

HELD IN THE

LECTURE ROOM

OF THE

ESSEX-STREET CHURCH, BOSTON,

Jan. 31, Feb. 8, 15, and 21, 1866.

BOSTON:
NICHOLS AND NOYES.
1866.

RESULT OF COUNCIL

HELD IN THE

LECTURE ROOM

OF THE

ESSEX-STREET CHURCH, BOSTON,

Jan. 31, Feb. 8, 15, and 21, 1866.

BOSTON:
NICHOLS AND NOYES.
1866.

Entered according to Act of Congress, in the year 1866, by

NICHOLS AND NOYES,

In the Clerk's Office of the District Court of the District of Massachusetts.

CAMBRIDGE:
STEREOTYPED AND PRINTED BY JOHN WILSON AND SONS.

LETTER MISSIVE.

BOSTON, Jan. 19, 1866.

To the *Church, Boston, with their Pastor,*
Rev. *the Union Church, Essex Street,*
Boston, sends greeting: —

DEAR CHRISTIAN BRETHREN, — You are aware that there seems to be a growing desire and expectation among us with regard to an increase of attention to the subject of personal salvation by Christ, and that Christians are consulting with one another as to the best ways of promoting it.

In former years, our Churches, with their Pastors, were accustomed to confer and act together with regard to the interests of religion in Boston. A united action on this subject serves to give strength to such measures as may be deemed desirable.

And whereas it is consonant with our Congregational usage that some one Church should take the first step when the Churches are invited to council together, and it having been suggested by some who are interested in this movement, that the Church whose Pastor has had the longest term of pastoral service in one Church could, with common assent, properly issue the Letter Missive for this purpose: —

We do, therefore, as a sister Church, affectionately invite you to be present, by your Pastor and *three* Delegates, at an Ecclesiastical Council, in the Lecture-room of this Church, on WEDNESDAY AFTERNOON, JANUARY THE THIRTY-FIRST, instant, at a *quarter past three* o'clock, to devise and recommend such practical measures as the Council may judge best adapted to extend a knowledge of salvation by our Lord Jesus Christ among the population of this city, and to impress the claims of the Gospel upon their consciences and hearts.

With cordial affection, your brethren in Christ,
In behalf of the Union Church,

N. ADAMS, *Pastor.*

DANIEL W. JOB, *Clerk (pro tem.).*

THE COUNCIL WILL CONSIST OF

THE ORTHODOX CONGREGATIONAL CHURCHES OF BOSTON, viz.: —

CHURCHES.	PASTORS.
OLD SOUTH	{ Rev. G. W. Blagden, D.D., and Rev. J. M. Manning.
PARK STREET	Rev. A. L. Stone, D.D.*
UNION	Rev. N. Adams, D.D.
PHILLIPS	Rev. E. K. Alden.
BERKELEY STREET	Rev. H. M. Dexter, D.D.
SALEM	Rev. S. P. Fay, Acting Pastor.
MARINERS'	
CENTRAL	Rev. J. E. Todd.
MAVERICK	Rev. J. S. Bingham.
MOUNT VERNON	Rev. E. N. Kirk, D.D.
SHAWMUT	Rev. E. B. Webb, D.D.
SPRINGFIELD STREET	
E STREET	Rev. A. R. Baker, Acting Pastor.
CHAMBERS STREET	{ Rev. G. W. Blagden, D.D., and Rev. J. M. Manning.

* Rev. Dr. Stone having resigned the pastoral charge of the Park-street Church, subject to the action of a Council, he is hereby invited as an honorary member, in the event of his dismission.

RESULT.

PURSUANT to letters missive of which the foregoing was the form, the Congregational Churches of Boston met in Council, by their Pastors and specified number of Delegates, at the appointed time and place, for the purpose of considering the state of religion, and devising and recommending practical measures for the furtherance of the Gospel in this city; and having held several sessions of a deeply devotional as well as a deliberative character, and having listened to important reports of committees appointed to set forth the defects in our religious condition, their causes and their remedies, — and having heard these subjects freely remarked upon and discussed, — and having humbly and earnestly sought the Divine guidance, — came to the following

RESULT.

For the feelings among Christians which led to the call of this Council, — for our assembling,

— for the spiritual interest and power of our sessions, increasing to their close, — and for the influence of these things upon the Churches, manifest and already extensive, — we are profoundly grateful to the Head of the Church.

We feel that in these things some of the true purposes of this Council have been already accomplished.

What further measures for the promotion of a deeper and more extensive religious interest among us may be expedient, is an important but difficult question. Different measures are suited to different times, and to Churches and neighborhoods of different character and condition; and therefore we are compelled to pass by many measures which are not of general applicability, and do not meet with universal approval.

We call the attention of the Churches to the imperative duty of entering upon new and more earnest courses of action. We are beset on the one side by rationalism and infidelity, on the other side by superstition, on every side by worldliness, ungodliness and vice. Multitudes around us, including many united to us by the strongest ties, are without any interest in the

Saviour, and are, therefore, in the way to everlasting ruin. At the same time, wordliness has crept into our Churches, the love of many has grown cold, and a wicked and fatal indifference and inactivity has paralyzed their energies.

We do, therefore, by their love of Christ, by their compassion for the perishing, by their hope of salvation, affectionately and solemnly adjure our Churches to employ such prompt, new and decided measures for the advance of the kingdom of Christ in and around them, as the Spirit of Christ which is in each shall suggest; and we do affectionately and solemnly adjure each of our Church members to enter at once upon a deeper and more thorough humiliation and repentance before God, a more entire separation of heart and life from the world, and a more faithful and earnest personal activity in the work of saving souls.

We feel that our first duty is, to point out affectionately but very plainly, some of the causes of this coldness, indifference and inactivity which we all so deeply deplore.

We all acknowledge the general truth, that if there is ever to be a revival in a Church, it must commence in the hearts of its members. We cannot hope for God's blessing upon the meetings and the prayers of nominal Christians who are daily sinning against their Maker, and whose daily lives are devoted to the service of mammon; such prayers are empty forms, without reverence, or love, or faith.

The sins of individual Christians are the cause of this condition of the Churches of Christ. While we rejoice to know and to acknowledge the unaffected piety, the simple faith and holy lives of so many Christians, we are also aware that the most earnest and the most devoted are those who are most alarmed at the general condition of the Churches.

There are many of the nominal members of the Churches of Christ whose daily lives are at war with the plain commands of the Gospel. Do they love God supremely? Are their affections set upon heavenly things? They do not endeavor to renounce the sinful customs and vanities of this world; but they allow the solemn realities of religion to become secondary to the duties and pleasures of the passing hour. Parents neglect family worship and faithful religious instruction in their families; they disregard the eternal welfare and the salvation of the immortal souls of their children, and make their duties to God subordinate to the friendships, the claims, the pleasures and the frivolities of social life. Trifling causes, which do not keep the lovers of pleasure from theatres and balls and parties, are sufficient to prevent nominal Christians from attending the services of God's sanctuary and the weekly meetings for prayer.

Prominent among the evils with regard to which there can be no trifling and no compromise, are two. We refer to the neglect of daily secret prayer and of the daily study of God's Word.

We desire to express our settled conviction, that daily secret prayer (not a formal lip service, but a real and consecrated communion with our Heavenly Father,) is as essential to a true Christian life as vital air is to the life of the body; and that a daily study of the Bible, with prayer for God's blessing upon the study of His own Word, is indispensable to growth in grace, and, indeed, to any really religious life. We have reason to believe that both of these vital points are daily neglected, to the endangering of many souls.

In connection with these duties we wish to bring forward into prominent view one great cause of the want of progress in the Church of Christ on earth. This is, that with but comparatively few exceptions, our members are not working for the cause of Christ and His kingdom.

What different results we might expect if every Christian were earnestly at work for the saving of souls! We believe that this is a plain Christian duty which cannot be neglected or evaded, that it is essential to a true Christian life, and that the only truly happy Christians are always working Christians.

RECOMMENDATIONS.

RENEWAL OF COVENANT.

In view of the painful declension in the Churches, and of the solemn responsibilities of this hour, when all around us we can hear of the coming power and glory of God, we do solemnly and earnestly recommend to each one of you, our Christian brethren and sisters, that you study carefully, and with earnest prayer, your covenant with God. Your conscience will instruct you as to your fidelity to the vows which you once took upon yourself in the presence of God and of His holy angels. If you feel that you have broken your covenant and neglected your duties, you *must* return, as a penitent sinner, to the one strait and narrow way. You *must* humble yourself before your Maker, and repent, and seek forgiveness and mercy through the atoning sacrifice of Christ, until you receive that free pardon which He gives to all who in sincerity and humility come to Him; and *then* you will be enabled by a sincere and heartfelt reconsecration of yourself to Christ, to become a living member of the Church to which you now are an occasion of grief and reproach. We know that this reconsecration is possible to every individual Christian, not as an empty form, nor by any public profession only, but after sincere self-humiliation, and a new pardon, and a glad reconciliation with God.

In order that this individual duty of humiliation and repentance, and of a new consecration to the service and glory of God may, in the most solemn manner, be brought home to the heart and conscience of every Christian, we recommend that all our Churches should simultaneously, on the third Sabbath of March, solemnly renew their covenant with God and with each other, and that this day should be devoted by every Christian to conscientious and searching self-examination, and to sincere humiliation before God. In order that this reconsecration may be general and effectual, we suggest that early notice should be given so far as possible, to every member of the Churches, and that one or more appropriate sermons be preached in each Church on or before the appointed day.

UNION COMMUNION.

We recommend also that in the evening of this day there should be united communion services in the Park-street Church, designed solely for the members of the Churches represented in this Council, in which they may join in token of their brotherly love, and union in Christ, as well as to seek the Divine blessing upon their solemn vows of reconsecration to the service and glory of God.

ADDRESSES TO CHURCH MEMBERS.

In order that the dangers and temptations to which Christians are exposed, the causes of coldness in our Churches, and the means through which we hope for a renewal of the work of the Holy Spirit among us, may be plainly set before the members of our Churches, we recommend that addresses by the Pastors be prepared and printed for distribution in every Church, upon the following subjects:

1. The Duty of a More Strict Observance of the Sabbath, by Rev. Dr. BLAGDEN.
2. The Power and Office of the Holy Spirit, by Rev. Dr. ADAMS.
3. The Power of Prayer, by Rev. Dr. KIRK.
4. The Christian's Reconsecration, by Rev. Mr. ALDEN.
5. The Worldliness of Nominal Christians, by Rev. Dr. WEBB.
6. The Spread of the Gospel in the City among the Poor and those who habitually neglect the Services of the Sabbath, by Rev. Dr. DEXTER.
7. The Christian's Duty to work for the Saving of Souls, by Rev. Mr. BINGHAM.
8. Revivals of Religion, by Rev. Mr. TODD.

9. The Duty of Daily Secret Prayer and Daily Study of the Bible, by Rev. Mr. MANNING.

10. The Duty of Christians to unite with some Church, and the Duty of Church Members to unite with the Church where they statedly worship, by Rev. Mr. FAY.

11. The Divine Sovereignty in its Relation to Human Salvation, by Rev. Mr. BAKER.

OBSERVANCE OF THE SABBATH.

We are convinced that the services of the Lord's Day ought to be considered *supreme* above all other times and means of grace. The members of our Churches should keep God's Sabbaths holy, and reverence His sanctuary by attending on both the services usually held. We know that these great duties are too much neglected.

PREACHING.

We believe that it is desirable that the Pastors should select subjects for their sermons such as the present hour seems to demand: and we recommend great plainness and distinctness in preaching upon those grand and solemn doctrines of the Bible: Man's total alienation from God; the Divine justice in the eternal punishment of the wicked; the new birth; salvation through faith in Christ.

These primal truths of God's Word, and Christ's stern and awful warnings against a nominal and merely formal worship of God should be preached afresh without any compromises with pride, heresy or worldliness; and God's ministers should be sustained and supported by Christians in this high duty.

UNION AMONG CHURCHES.

We recommend that every means should be taken to bring about a more fraternal union and practical sympathy and co-operation between all our Churches in the city. A more familiar intercourse and more frequent associations will bring about these desirable results. Mutual regard and respect and acquaintance should be cultivated, in every manner, and as some of the means to insure these objects, we recommend: combined or union prayer meetings; informal delegations of members from one Church to another at the usual social meetings; united public services as occasion may offer; occasional unions in the communion services; and more frequent exchanges among the Pastors.

PRAYER FOR THE HOLY SPIRIT.

We need a higher faith in the prevailing power of prayer. If the five thousand members of our Churches were awakened to the solemn responsibilities of the present moment, and were all united in fervent daily prayers for God's blessing, we should not require councils, or need to suggest reforms.

We therefore earnestly adjure all who love the Lord Jesus Christ that they do daily, with deep earnestness and trusting faith, strive earnestly in prayer for the manifest presence and power of the Holy Spirit in all our Churches.

EXTRA MEETINGS.

We are disposed to believe that much of the force and efficiency of the Sabbath services is lost because the hearers during the week are given up to the world, and the solemn impressions of the Sabbath are effaced. We therefore recommend that each Church should increase the number of its social prayer meetings: and that for the present these meetings should usually be devoted to prayers for the Holy Spirit and for the conversion of the impenitent. We suggest also that increased efforts should be made by Christians to induce the unconverted to attend these meetings.

GENERAL VISITATION.

We recommend that in each Church competent and experienced Christians shall be appointed to visit the members, for the purpose of conversing with them on the subject of personal religion, for their mutual profit. In this way the hearts of true Christians may be encouraged and quickened, and the unfaithful may be won back to duty and their first love. It would be well for the visitors to go forth two and two, as the Lord appointed, a few members of the Church being assigned to each pair. Simultaneous neighborhood prayer meetings, or a special Church meeting might profitably close the work.

SPECIAL AND PROTRACTED MEETINGS.

The subject of special meetings in the daytime during the week, and of protracted meetings, seems to depend so much upon the spiritual state, and the situation in other respects, of our several Churches, that we think it best to make this suggestion only,—that whenever any Church shall appoint such meetings, it is the duty of all sister Churches, so far as it may be convenient, to co-operate sincerely, and assist them.

SABBATH SCHOOLS.

We recommend a more general and faithful attendance upon the Sabbath Schools, especially on the part of adults. Every member of our congregations, and especially every Christian, for whom it is possible, should be connected with some Sabbath School, as a teacher or a scholar. The Sabbath School ought to be employed as a means of drawing children and others into the services of the sanctuary, and not as an independent and superior instrumentality of grace. We suggest also, that the Sabbath School should be made less a means of merely interesting and amusing the children, and more a means of instructing them and bringing them to Christ; and that every Sabbath School teacher is bound to use the most diligent and faithful efforts to bring the children to a personal interest in the Saviour.

CITY MISSIONARY SOCIETY.

We recommend a more earnest attention on the part of every Church to the wants and claims of the City Missionary Society. The number of missionaries needs to be increased; and the means of enabling them to minister temporal relief, as it opens a direct road for the Gospel to the hearts of the suffering, should be liberally supplied. Every Church ought to have missionaries of its own employed under the general direction of this Society.

LAY PREACHERS.

If any Church can procure from among its own members, or elsewhere, suitable men to preach Christ in mission chapels, halls, or vestries, as lay preachers under the supervision and with the co-operation of the Pastor, we earnestly recommend the employment of such assistance.

NEW CHURCHES, ETC.

In view of the dense and neglected population in the north part of the city, it would be obviously unfaithful to the Master, should our

Churches cease to maintain vigorously our faith and polity in that part of the city; while the rapid growth of the city, in our judgment, requires the immediate erection of a new meeting-house and the consequent organization of a new Church of our order at the extreme South End, and also at East Boston.

DISTRICTING THE CITY.

We believe that the apportionment of the city into districts, and the assignment of a district to each Church for its religious care, is already in progress. We recommend each church to accept the field of labor which shall be offered it, and enter with alacrity and vigor upon the work. The religious condition of every family should be known; and not a child unconnected with any Sabbath School should be left unsought; not a stranger in the city should be left to its temptations and snares, uncaught by a Christian hand; and not an individual should be permitted to pass through and out of life, within the bounds of the district, without having distinctly and repeatedly presented to him, the knowledge and offers of Christ's salvation.

Such a work will call for much self-denying labor on the part of the whole Church; and we do, in the most solemn manner, and by the most sacred considerations, urge the Churches to come up heartily to the work. Let every Christian feel that there is something for him, or her, to do. Let some work be assigned to each, according to his or her several ability. Let every Christian remember, that not only among the poor and lost, but at home and by the way, in business circles and among his friends, he is under the strongest obligations to preach Christ, with modesty, wisdom, meekness and love, not only by his works but with his lips.

ENCOURAGEMENT TO LABOR.

We call the attention of the Churches to the fact that at the present time we have special encouragement to labor. There seems to be a readiness in the minds of men to listen to the Gospel. There seems to be a general expectation of an unusual outpouring of the Spirit. All around us showers of grace are falling. In all of our Churches there is an element of faithfulness and prayer; in some of them there is an unusually tender and solemn state of feeling. In our own sessions and their influence we believe that we have seen indications that the Lord is with us, and going before us.

Let us, then, Pastors and Churches, awake to the responsibilities and privileges of the hour. The time is short; the reward is great; and lo! Christ is with us alway.

Addresses to Church Members

Are in preparation, as follows, viz.: —

1. The Duty of a more Strict Observance of the Sabbath, by Rev. Dr. BLAGDEN.
2. The Power and Office of the Holy Spirit, by Rev. Dr. ADAMS.
3. The Power of Prayer, by Rev. Dr. KIRK.
4. The Christian's Reconsecration, by Rev. Mr. ALDEN.
5. The Worldliness of Nominal Christians, by Rev. Dr. WEBB.
6. The Spread of the Gospel in the City among the Poor and those who habitually neglect the Services of the Sabbath, by Rev. Dr. DEXTER.
7. The Christian's Duty to work for the Saving of Souls, by Rev. Mr. BINGHAM.
8. Revivals of Religion, by Rev. Mr. TODD.
9. The Duty of Daily Secret Prayer and Daily Study of the Bible, by Rev. Mr. MANNING.
10. The Duty of Christians to unite with some Church, and the Duty of Church Members to unite with the Church where they statedly worship, by Rev. Mr. FAY.
11. The Divine Sovereignty in its Relation to Human Salvation, by Rev. Mr. BAKER.

In accordance with the recommendation of the Council, the Addresses named above will be printed without delay, for the purpose suggested. The first of the series, by Rev. Mr. ALDEN, will be issued in a few days.

THE

CHRISTIAN'S RECONSECRATION.

By REV. E. K. ALDEN.

BOSTON:
NICHOLS AND NOYES.
1866.

THE

CHRISTIAN'S RECONSECRATION.

By REV. E. K. ALDEN.

BOSTON:
NICHOLS AND NOYES.
1866.

Entered according to Act of Congress, in the year 1866, by

NICHOLS AND NOYES,

In the Clerk's Office of the District Court of the District of Massachusetts.

CAMBRIDGE:
STEREOTYPED AND PRINTED BY JOHN WILSON AND SONS.

THE

CHRISTIAN'S RECONSECRATION.

Upon the twelfth day of January, 1723, Jonathan Edwards, being then nineteen years of age, wrote the following words: " I have this day solemnly renewed my baptismal covenant and self-dedication, which I renewed when I was received into the communion of the Church. I have been before God; and have given myself, all that I am and have, to God, so that I am not in any respect my own: I can claim no right in myself, no right in this understanding, this will, these affections that are in me; neither have I any right to this body, or any of its members; no right to this tongue, these hands, or feet; no right to these senses, these eyes, these ears, this smell, or taste. I have given myself clear away, and have not retained any thing as my own. I have been to God this morning, and told Him that I gave myself *wholly* to Him. I have given every power to Him; so that, for the future, I will challenge or claim no right in myself in any respect. I have this morning told Him that I did take Him for my whole portion and felicity, looking on nothing else as any part of my happiness, nor acting as if it were; and His law as the constant rule of my obedience; and would fight with all my might against the world, the flesh, and the devil, to the end of my life. And did believe in Jesus Christ, and receive Him as a Prince and a Saviour; and would adhere to the faith and obedience of the Gospel, how hazardous and difficult soever the profession and practice of it may be. That I did receive the blessed Spirit as my Teacher, Sanctifier, and only Comforter; and cherish all His motions to enlighten, purify, confirm, comfort and assist me. This I have done. And I pray God, for the sake of Christ, to look upon it as a self-dedication; and to receive me now as entirely His own, and deal with me in all respects as such, whether He afflicts me or prospers me, or whatever He pleases to do with me who am His. Now henceforth I am not to act in any respect as my own. I shall act as my own, if I ever make use of any of my powers to any thing that is not to the glory of God, or do not make the glorifying of Him my whole and entire business; if I murmur in the least at afflictions; if I grieve at the prosperity of others; if I am in any way uncharitable; if I am angry because of injuries; if I revenge my own cause; if I do any thing purely to please myself, or avoid any thing for the sake of my ease, or omit any thing because it is great self-denial; if I trust to myself; if I take any of the praise of any good that I do, or, rather, God does by me; or if I am any way proud. . . . Resolved, frequently to renew the dedication of myself to God, which was made at my baptism, and which I solemnly renewed when I was received into the communion of the Church; and which I have solemnly ratified this twelfth day of January, 1723. Resolved, never to act as if I were any way my own, but entirely and altogether God's."

Upon the twenty-fifth of July, 1805, Edward Payson, being upon that day twenty-two years of age, wrote the following words: " Having resolved this day to dedicate myself to my Creator, in a serious and solemn manner, by a written covenant, I took a review of my past life, and of the numerous mercies by which it has been distinguished. Then, with sincerity as I humbly hope, I took the Lord to be my God, and engaged to love, serve, and obey Him. Relying on the assistance of His Holy Spirit, I engaged to take the Holy Scriptures as the rule of my conduct, the Lord Jesus Christ to be my Saviour, and the Spirit of all grace and consolation as my Guide and Sanctifier. The vows of God are on me." Upon the first of May, 1807, he renewed this dedication of himself to God in a solemn Confession and form of Covenant, closing thus: "As a testimony of my sincere and hearty consent to this covenant, of my hope and desire to see the blessings of it, and as a swift witness against me if I depart from it, I do now, before God and the holy angels, subscribe with my hands unto the Lord.—*Edward Payson.* . . . And may this covenant be ratified in Heaven! And do thou remember, O my soul! that the vows of God are upon thee. . . . Having drawn up the above covenant, I spread it before the Lord; and, after confession of sins, and seeking pardon through the blood of

Christ, I did solemnly accept it before Him, as my free act and deed; and embraced Christ in it as the only ground of my hope."

These are illustrations of a Christian's reconsecration, a practical commentary upon the apostolic precepts: "I beseech you, therefore, brethren, by the mercies of God, that ye present your bodies a living sacrifice, holy, acceptable unto God, which is your reasonable service. . . . Yield yourselves unto God as those that are alive from the dead, and your members as instruments of righteousness unto God. . . . Know ye not that your body is the temple of the Holy Ghost, Which is in you, Which ye have of God, and ye are not your own? For ye are bought with a price: therefore, glorify God in your body and in your spirit, which are God's."

Reconsecration supposes a first consecration. There was a time when, as an anxious sinner oppressed with a sense of guilt and peril, despairing of human help, you beheld the Lamb of God who taketh away the sin of the world; you accepted Him as a personal Redeemer, you recognized His claim to your entire being, and you dedicated yourself to His service. That hallowed hour may be but recent in your experience, or it may be that for many years you have been active in various departments of Christian usefulness; you have enjoyed continuous and comforting evidence that you are a child of God, or, perhaps, your mind has been at times perplexed and darkened; you have maintained a consistent Christian deportment in the eyes of your fellow-men, or, possibly, the fervor of your first love may have declined, and you have been led astray by the corruptions of your own heart, and the temptations of the world. Whatever and wherever you now may be in the Christian pilgrimage, permit me to suggest for your candid consideration the value of a solemn personal act of reconsecration to the Lord Jesus Christ.

I. There are some Christians in whose early experience the idea of consecration is not prominent. They believe in Christ as a Saviour through whom they receive forgiveness of sins and adoption into the household of God. They know, in some measure, the peace of those who are justified by faith, and rejoice in the hope of the glory of God. But they do not, with the same definiteness, apprehend Christ as their Master, to Whom they belong, and in Whose service they dedicate their entire energies to practical personal obedience. This thought does not thoroughly take posssession of their souls, and decide the conduct of their lives. They are not conscious of a distinct renunciation of the world, deliberately forsaking all its attractions, and choosing a life of self-denial, as disciples of Christ. They may live many years, knowing at times genuine Christian emotion and affection; and yet may not thoroughly surrender every thing to the service of Christ, and enter vigorously upon the Christian work. Some are puzzled and perplexed by the call to an entire dedication of thought, purpose, energy, time, property, business, every thing, to Christ, and confess to themselves and to others that they do not understand what it means. They are conscious that it is, in many of its aspects, a new question, and that they have never fully grappled with its requirements. But, as the question begins to present itself in its true significance, and they perceive its fundamental nature, and become aware that it is searching to the innermost motive of their hearts, not unfrequently their whole religious experience is upheaved by it,— they take the question up prayerfully and conscientiously in the fear of God; and when, yielding to its claims, they do indeed dedicate their entire being practically and for ever to the service of Christ, the act marks in their history a new and momentous era.

II. There are some who begin the Christian life with a definite act of self-dedication to God, but who fail to retain the idea as an influential power amid the exposures of the world. Of the multitudes awakened to serious thought, who have read "The Rise and Progress of Religion in the Soul," by Philip Doddridge, not a few, endeavoring in all simplicity to follow his directions, have paused as they concluded the seventeenth chapter, and then and there for themselves have transcribed and signed some form of "self-dedication to the service of God." They have done it with seriousness and prayer, and have never forgotten the impressions of the hour. Probably something of this style of dedication has been known by a considerable number of persons who have been hopefully converted during childhood or early youth. Occasionally, there is one who records that he signs this private covenant of his soul with God with his own blood. The years roll on, and this young, ardent disciple has gone forth to his work in life, determined to be entirely dedicated to the service of Christ, according to the spirit of the covenant into which he has entered with the Father, the Son, and the Holy Ghost. But he finds that he has very feebly comprehended what those solemn words included; that it is quite a different matter in youth, in the solitude of private meditation, to transcribe such a covenant, and to sign it upon the knees before God, and in mature years, amid all the exposures of earth's ambition and wealth, to observe that covenant in daily life and conversation. There are some, indeed, who never give over this purpose; who hold themselves steadily to their vows during all their days; and who frequently renew their consecration, with a clearer apprehension of its meaning and with increasing solemnity, to the end of life. But it is a fact to which many will testify in sadness, that the personal dedication which they made to God in the days of their youthful religious fervor, long since lost its practical power in their Christian experience. "The cares of the world, the deceitfulness of riches, and the lusts of other things, entering in have choked the word, and it has become unfruitful." The glow of tender personal love to Christ has passed away. They have not cherished the thought of His presence as they have journeyed along their pilgrimage. They have been living, in a great degree, for themselves, consulting their own ease and convenience, turning aside from the path of daily self-denial, gradually conforming to the world, ceasing the strenuous endeavor to be entirely free from sin and entirely godly in heart and life, until by and by, awakened in the midst of their days to consider where they are in the Christian life, they find themselves absorbed in selfish and worldly plans; and the idea of an entire self-dedication to the service of God, into which they once entered with alacrity, is well-nigh appalling to them. They wonder how they ever subscribed to such a covenant, and are almost ready to protest against the act as sacrilege. As they apprehend it now, its significance becomes awful. They begin to reason with themselves, and ask, Does every thing I have belong to God? Am I only a steward using God's property sacredly for His service? Am I living, speaking, transacting business, regulating all my affairs on that principle? If this is the test of Christian discipleship, what is my evidence of piety worth? Some refuse to yield to the searching power of such questions as these, administering to themselves a delusive comfort in the hasty assertion, that entire consecration is an impossibility, and need not be attempted; but others bow down beneath this startling revelation of their own selfishness and pride, submit themselves to the word which pierces even to the dividing asunder of soul and spirit, cry earnestly to God for mercy, mourn bitterly as they meet the eye of the Saviour they have grieved, and at length know in their own experience the priceless worth of a genuine reconsecration.

III. There are some striving to follow on to know the Lord, who become conscious that their practical ideal of the Christian life is changing, their views are enlarging, they are hungering and thirsting for a type of Christian experience to which they have not yet attained, and which yet seems attainable: they want, as far as it can be known on earth, the full liberty of a child of God; and they find themselves in prayer, meditation, and Christian labor, perpetually impelled toward the endeavor to be consciously and entirely Christ's, "body, soul, and spirit." As one of the helps in this direction, they learn, perhaps after protracted and weary struggles, that there is a wondrous power, while in this attitude of thought, in appropriating the Lord Jesus Christ as an atoning Saviour *anew*, in recognizing God's right to all we have and are *anew*, in receiving in a special sense the personal anointing of the Holy Ghost *anew*, and in accepting the fulness of promises, as they are dawning upon the illumined soul in a richer and more glorious significance, *anew*.

"Resolved," writes Edwards, "to improve every opportunity when I am in my best and happiest frame of mind, to cast and venture my soul on the Lord Jesus Christ; to trust and confide in Him, and consecrate myself wholly to Him." — "In order to maintain this habitual delightful sense of God," writes Doddridge, "I would frequently renew my dedication to Him, in that covenant on which all my hopes depend, and my resolutions for universal zealous obedience. I will study redeeming love more, and habitually resign myself and all my concerns to the Divine disposal. . . . O blessed Spirit! graciously descend on my polluted heart. Strike the flint, O thou almighty arm of the Lord! that the waters may flow forth. I come to humble myself before God; I come to renew my resolutions against sin; I come to refer my concerns to Him; I come to seal my engagements to be the Lord's." This is the man who wrote the familiar hymn, whose final stanza begins, —

> "High Heaven that heard the solemn vow,
> *That vow renewed shall daily hear.*"

Whitefield writes, in the maturity of his life, after long years of fervent laborious service for Christ, "I intend, by God's assistance, *now to begin;* for as yet, alas! I have done nothing. Oh that I may *begin in earnest!* God quicken my tardy pace, and help me to do much work in little time!"

Occasionally it is an epoch in the Christian life from which some believers date a remarkable change in the joyous consciousness of their souls, when after a painful strife for entire consecration *to* Christ, at length, with all simplicity of faith, they receive a consecration *from* Christ: when yielding to what they perceive are His acknowledged claims, they hear Him saying, "Ye have not chosen Me, but I have chosen you, and *ordained* you, that ye should go and bring forth fruit, and that your fruit should remain. . . . As My Father hath sent Me, so send I you." Calvin, in his Commentary on the First Epistle of John, exclaims, "I have not sued Thee by my love, O Christ! Thou hast loved me of Thy free will. Thou hast shone into my soul, and then every thing that dazzled my eyes by a false splendor immediately disappeared, or at least I take no count of it." Here the Christian's reconsecration and his re-acceptance of the unsearchable riches of Christ sweetly blend together; and what is regarded as that difficult act of self-abdication is found to be a precious act of childlike faith, leading into all the joy and peace of believing. This idea is finely illustrated in the account, given by President Edwards, of the remarkable transports of one whose fresh experience, though she had been a devoted Christian for twenty-seven years, he thus relates: "They began near three years ago, in a great increase, in *an extraordinary self-dedication and renunciation of the world and resignation of all to God,* made in a great view of God's excellency, and high exercise of love to Him, and rest and joy in Him, . . . and began in a yet higher degree, about a year and a half ago, upon *another new resignation of all to God,* with a yet greater fervency and delight of soul, . . . and began in a much higher degree still, the last winter, upon *another resignation and acceptance of God,* as the only portion and happiness of the soul, wherein the whole world, with the dearest enjoyments in it, were renounced as dirt and dung; and all that is pleasant and glorious, and all that is terrible in this world, seemed perfectly to vanish into nothing; and nothing to be left but God, in Whom the soul was perfectly swallowed up as in an infinite ocean of blessedness." Is there such a self-dedication of the soul to God as this? Are there such reconsecrations of the already renewed and partially sanctified believer as these, followed by " a constant sweet peace and calm and serenity of soul, without any cloud to interrupt it, . . . a wonderful access to God by prayer, as it were seeing Him, and sensibly, immediately conversing with Him ; as much, oftentimes, as if Christ were here upon earth, . . . all sorrow and sighing fled away, except grief for past sins and for remaining corruption, and that Christ is loved no more, and that God is no more honored in the world, and a compassionate grief toward fellow-creatures, a daily sensible doing and suffering every thing for God, . . . doing all as the service of love, and so doing it with a continual, uninterrupted cheerfulness, peace and joy?" Well may we exclaim, with the narrator of this experience, "If such things are enthusiasm and the fruits of a distempered brain, let my brain be evermore possessed of that happy distemper! If this be distraction, I pray God that the world of mankind may be all seized with this benign, meek, beneficent, beatifical, glorious distraction!"

It does not become one Christian believer to mark out the precise method in which another shall for himself perform this solemn act of personal reconsecration to God. The method will differ according to the constitutional temperament and external circumstances of each individual, and will also be modified by peculiarities of past religious experience. Let each one select his own method. It may be by means of some written form of covenant signed and sealed as in the Divine presence; it may be by making an inventory of all one has and is, and specifically dedicating property, business, time, reading, recreation,* family, person, body, and mind to God; it may be in the forgetting of what is behind, and a new and full acceptance of Christ as all in all; it may be in connection with agonizing supplication; it may be in simple, quiet trust: but in some form let it be a transaction between each individual and God, — the genuine outpouring of the soul with the sincerity of one meeting his Lord face to face, and henceforth knowing Him in the fellowship of a loved and loving child.

Come then, O longing disciple! not merely to make a consecration, but also to receive a consecration. Your Lord and Master is setting you apart anew for His own work, and will bestow upon you of His own fullness. For it is the blessedness of yielding up all to God, that henceforth you receive all from God; and, if you are His, He also is yours. Not, then, with timid and

---

* "Let me consecrate my sleep and all my recreations to God, and seek them for his sake." — *Doddridge.*

hesitating steps, but with joyous thanksgivings, amazed at our own sinful distrust, hastening to fall down penitently and confess our sin, hastening to receive the Divine benediction waiting to be bestowed upon us, let us now approach the altar of our God, blessing Him that it is our privilege, with a clearer apprehension of the significance of the act, to present our bodies a living sacrifice, holy, acceptable unto God, which is our reasonable service.

Almighty God! Whose I am by creation, preservation, and redemption, I do now bow before Thee, a sinner utterly unworthy, renouncing self, appropriating anew to my own soul the blood of the atonement; accepting anew the Lord Jesus Christ as the way, the truth, and the life; acknowledging Thee, Father, Son, and Holy Spirit, as my gracious, ever-present God. I do now surrender every member of my body and every faculty of my mind to Thee, to be used by Thee as Thou shalt please. I give to Thee, without reservation, my time, my business, my earthly possessions, receiving all that Thou shalt bestow as a sacred trust to be employed in Thy service. To the extension of Thy kingdom in the world, to the salvation of my fellow-men, to the glory of Christ, my Saviour, I devote, with thankfulness of heart, all I have and am. I accept Thy blessing, Thy guidance, Thy constant presence, Holy Comforter, to be with me and in me evermore to the end. And as I now feel Thy hand, O Divine Redeemer, laid upon my head re-dedicating me to Thy service, *I accept the dedication.* " God forbid that I should glory, save in the cross of our Lord Jesus Christ, by Whom the world is crucified unto me, and I unto the world." — " THY VOWS ARE UPON ME, O GOD ! "

COVENANT.

[The following form of covenant has been prepared, by Rev. Dr. KIRK, on the basis of one which was written by President EDWARDS. It is inserted here for those who may desire to use such a form.]

IN the name of my God and Saviour, Who promises me strength for all my work, I hereby enter into this covenant.

Acknowledging my unworthiness and His infinite goodness; deeply lamenting my present unhappy distance from Him; fervently imploring the forgiveness of all my sins, and entreating for Christ's sake to be called a child of God, — I hereby renounce the world as my portion; all the pleasures, honors, and profits of sin; and take the Lord to be my portion and my Saviour.

I engage to make it my supreme design, to exalt God above all creatures in my own view, and in the view of all men.

I will endeavor evermore to stand upon the foundation God has laid in Zion, the person and work of the Lord Jesus Christ, as the ground of my peaceful relations with God.

I engage, in all my conversation and intercourse with others, to deal honestly, justly, and uprightly; never overreaching or defrauding in any matter, nor wilfully injuring them in their interest.

I engage to give no just cause of offence to any; either by negligently withholding from him his dues, or by speaking evil of him, or needlessly mentioning his faults, or by allowing a spirit of ill-will or any unkind feeling, or by maintaining a party spirit.

I engage to obey the Lord's command, "If thou bring thy gift to the altar, and there rememberest that thy brother hath aught against thee, leave there thy gift before the altar, and go thy way: first be reconciled to thy brother; and then come, and offer thy gift."

I engage to avoid all those pastimes, which, upon sober and prayerful consideration, seem to me inconsistent with a devout religious spirit and close walking with God.

I engage to promote, in myself and others, all generous, pure, heavenly dispositions; to walk in my house in the fear of the Lord.

I engage to put away, as far as is in my power, within me and around me, every thing that hinders my own growth in holiness and the conversion of others to God.

Cheerfully and gratefully I lay myself, and all I am

and own, at the feet of Him who redeemed me with His precious blood, engaging to follow Him, and bearing the cross He places upon me.

By this covenant I will frequently examine myself, and review my life; occasionally renewing it with prayer and fasting.

To God the Father, Son, and Holy Ghost, the God of grace and salvation, I hereby devote myself for time and eternity. *Amen.*

Addresses to Church Members

Are in preparation, as follows, viz.: —

1. The Duty of a more Strict Observance of the Sabbath, by Rev. Dr. BLAGDEN.
2. The Power and Office of the Holy Spirit, by Rev. Dr. ADAMS.
3. The Power of Prayer, by Rev. Dr. KIRK.
4. The Christian's Reconsecration, by Rev. Mr. ALDEN.
5. The Worldliness of Nominal Christians, by Rev. Dr. WEBB.
6. The Spread of the Gospel in the City among the Poor and those who habitually neglect the Services of the Sabbath, by Rev. Dr. DEXTER.
7. The Christian's Duty to work for the Saving of Souls, by Rev. Mr. BINGHAM.
8. Revivals of Religion, by Rev. Mr. TODD.
9. The Duty of Daily Secret Prayer and Daily Study of the Bible, by Rev. Mr. MANNING.
10. The Duty of Christians to unite with some Church, and the Duty of Church Members to unite with the Church where they statedly worship, by Rev. Mr. FAY.
11. The Divine Sovereignty in its Relation to Human Salvation, by Rev. Mr. BAKER.

In accordance with the recommendation of the Council, the Addresses named above will be printed without delay, for the purpose suggested. The first of the series, by Rev. Mr. ALDEN, will be issued in a few days.

THE WORLDLINESS

OF

NOMINAL CHRISTIANS.

BY

Rev. E. B. WEBB, D.D.

Published by Vote of the Congregational Council.

BOSTON:
NICHOLS AND NOYES.
1866.

THE WORLDLINESS

OF

NOMINAL CHRISTIANS.

BY

Rev. E. B. WEBB, D.D.

Published by Vote of the Congregational Council.

BOSTON:
NICHOLS AND NOYES.
1866.

Entered according to Act of Congress, in the year 1866, by

NICHOLS AND NOYES,

In the Clerk's Office of the District Court of the District of Massachusetts.

CAMBRIDGE:
STEREOTYPED AND PRINTED BY JOHN WILSON AND SONS.

Worldliness of Nominal Christians.

JOHN, writing to fathers and young men, uses this language, terse and decisive: "*Love not the world, neither the things that are in the world. If any man love the world, the love of the Father is not in him.*" Is there occasion for Christians now to take this stringent exhortation home to their own heart and life? and are we ready to apply a test so incisive and irresistible?

It seems to be taken for granted, that the members of our churches are worldly-minded. It is a root disease, blighting our strength, and repelling the Divine approaches. It is a guilty state, calling for self-scrutiny, immediate repentance, and practical reform. How many are willing to look into this matter, and determine what spirit they are of? Are you?

Let us see. Paul makes a clear, sharp distinction between the flesh and the Spirit: "To be carnally minded is death; but to be spiritually minded is life and peace." And the test he puts in this way: "They that are after the flesh do mind the things of the flesh; but they that are after the Spirit, the things of the Spirit." Now, we are not going into the street for evidence; nor into places of business, nor into places of pleasure, nor into circles of friendship, to note the conversation; nor into Christian homes, to learn, from the tastes and habits of the children, what is the dominant spirit of the parents. This might be very conclusive, and still very superficial. Let me put it and leave it to every one's own conscience: Say, brother, in the presence of God, and to Him who searches the heart, have you been spiritually minded or worldly-minded?

"No man can serve two masters."—"Ye cannot serve God and mammon." Either the love of the world or the love of God must be uppermost. And, if a man love the world, "how dwelleth the love of God in him?"

Paul puts the test still further: "But ye are

not in the flesh, but in the Spirit, if so be that the Spirit of God *dwell* in you." There is a difference between a *dwelling* and an *inn*. The one is a place for transient visitors; the other, a permanent abode, a home. Now, we have had a great many good thoughts during the last half-a-dozen years; but have our hearts been any thing more than an *inn*, into which they have entered and from which they have departed like transient visitors? Jesus was constrained to abide with the two disciples till they knew Him, and had a message for those at Jerusalem. Have you constrained Him to *abide* with you? Or is this all that you know, that He has occasionally passed by?

The *Comforter* was given expressly to "*abide*" with you for ever. You know how He lifts the soul into sympathy with Jesus; how the world seems but vanity and ashes, and the kingdom of heaven real and precious, when He is present. Has your heart been a home for the Comforter? Blessed companionship! happy home! Or does all this sound like talk about dreamland, or a vision of the future yet to be overtaken?

If further evidence of our want of the spiritual mind is required, we have it in the fact, that the peculiar, distinguishing doctrines of the gospel are *assented to* rather than believed. As a dead chieftain in the camp, they inspire no awe; as an opinion about the height of the Andes, they feed the strength of no supreme conviction. But these vital truths of the gospel, such as the guilt of all men; forgiveness only through faith in the blood of Christ crucified; native depravity, and regeneration by the Holy Ghost; a day of judgment; a final and eternal separation of the righteous and the wicked,— these are not dead theories, not the footballs of human speculation, but living truths for living men to confront and grapple with,— ay, rather, truths to be received in mastery of the conscience and will, heart and life, of every rational creature.

And not only these, but the *principles* which should govern our daily life are equally ignored, if not equally offensive. We are ready to soften down the doctrines, and indulge, with many plausible excuses, the desire for personal ease and sensual gratification. Jesus said unto his disciples, " If any man will come after me, let him *deny* himself, and take up his *cross* daily, and follow *me*." Now, where are the cross-bearers in this ease-loving, pleasure-seeking age? Are there none? yes, here and there one. But put the test just quoted, and put this further test: "If any man come to me, and hate not his father and mother and wife and children and brethren and sisters, yea, and his own life also, he cannot be my disciple." Do you really put your Saviour before yourself? Do you consciously subordinate all family considerations to the interests of Christ's kingdom? You may decide, if you will, what spirit you are of. Dear brethren, shall we fly from this subject to something more agreeable? or shall we tremblingly put the test, and abide the issue?

Still further, keeping to our own hearts, let us examine our *aims*. For what, for whom, are we living? You know the Scripture: "If ye be risen with Christ, seek those things which are above."—"Take no thought for the body, what ye shall eat, or what ye shall drink, or what ye shall put on, but"—think about this, do this,—"seek ye first the kingdom of God and His righteousness." Brethren, it is a fearful thing not to be in sympathy with Jesus. Are we aiming at his ends? "Lay not up for yourselves treasures upon earth, but lay up for yourselves treasures in heaven." Now, brother, have you not been devoted for some years past, mind and heart, to material possessions and worldly pleasures? Can you claim confidence in your self-knowledge, and admit any thing else? If, in all this struggling and crowding and jostling, you have been aiming to advance the cause of Christ, and, in a spirit of self-denial, serenely laying up treasure in heaven, God be praised; but have you?

We do not suppose that Christians are guilty of gross sins or inconsistencies. We take it for granted that they avoid all sharp practice, and doubtful indulgences, and open selfishness. But he who goes no further than this has a most imperfect idea of Christ, and of the believer's relation to Him. He who stops with the outward, has not even approached the Divine life; and "knows nothing as he ought to know it."

And now let us turn to look at some of the consequences of worldliness:—

1. It excites the displeasure of the Lord Jesus Christ. When the Lord talked to Peter about

going to Jerusalem and suffering at the hands of the chief priests and elders, and about being killed, and raised again on the third day, that disciple would change the subject, and avoid the predictions. But the Lord, whose heart was set on the prosperity of His kingdom, though it must prosper through self-denial and self-sacrifice, was offended with Peter, and turned His face from him with this rebuke: " Thou savorest not the things that be of God, but those that be of men." To enjoy Christ's favor, we must have His spirit. To share His fellowship, we must share his purposes. Napoleon once said, " Jerusalem is not in the line of my operations." But, if we would stand in the presence of Jesus, and enjoy His face, we must be ready to sympathize with Him in all His expectations, and go wherever He shall lead. What can compensate for the displeasure of the Lord?

2. Another result of worldliness is an utter want of confidence in the use and efficacy of the simple, essential truths of the gospel. To suffer, to die, " that be far from Thee, Lord." To rely upon the doctrines, to resort to prayer, to expect the presence and conscious influence of the Holy

Ghost, " that be far from our confidence," is the practical testimony of the nominal Christian. And, instead, he relies upon mere human talent or influence or eloquence to advance the cause of Christ, and resorts to mere worldly contrivances, and panders to a depraved popular taste. As well advance the spring, and loose the streams, and clothe the valleys with golden harvests, with a fire of brush and a garden hose. How can one have confidence in spiritual powers and persons, when he has lost all spiritual perception and affinity? How can his interest be any thing but transient, or his experience any thing but shallow?

3. Another effect of worldly-mindedness is ignorance of the Holy Spirit's special presence. It must be a poetic mind to recognize the poet. It requires a spiritual mind to recognize the Spirit's presence. Christ agonized in the garden, but the disciples had not sympathy enough with Him to keep awake. He came and stood beside them, and bent over them, with words on His tongue that would have thrilled their hearts and gladdened all their future; but they were ignorant and unconscious of His presence. And that

was a lost opportunity, a loss never to be made up, an occasion never to be repeated. Just so, within the last few years, the Spirit has been present again and again, — present to open the Scriptures, present to quicken and comfort and convert the soul; but worldliness has held every sense fast locked in sleep. "Oh that thou hadst known the times of thy visitation!" Brethren, is it not "high time to awake out of sleep," and listen for the sound of descending wings?

4. Another effect of worldly mindedness is, that the believer is obliged to go over the whole question of his own conversion every time the Spirit is really poured out. While all are in the dark together, one man's foundation is as good as another. But, as soon as the light begins to shine, the worldly mind is in trouble. Thoughts, affections, aspirations, have been elsewhere; and now a painful want, a miserable uncertainty, is revealed. Of course, such a Christian can do no good. He has no strength, no confidence in himself. Like a beam of light, severed from the sun, separated from Christ, his light is darkness. He has no voice, no burden of prayer, for others; all his anxiety is to hear for himself, "Thy

sins be forgiven thee." And thus it is, over and over again, every time the Spirit is forced upon him.

5. And hence another result is very few additions to the Church. And even those who suppose themselves converted find so little difference between the Church and the world, that they can hardly decide to change their relation. On the other hand, the young from Christian families are brought over to card-playing and wine-drinking; children spend their sabbaths, or a portion of them, where they are taught to call their fathers' faith illiberal, bigoted, puritanic; operas flourish, theatres multiply, and Christians relax their watchfulness and yield to the magnetism of pleasure, and follow their children. Behold the result! The Church as impotent as a debating society; the sharp gratifications of sense sought and enjoyed, instead of the fruits of the Spirit and the peace of God in the soul; Zion trailing her beautiful garments in the dust; and almost no conversions from the world. Again and again, the atmosphere of our worshipping assemblies seems agitated, as by the emotions of the Divine heart; but it is as when the sunshine and the

dew visit the rock. There is no springing foliage, no fruit. To be sure, there are, here and there, conversions among us, and, from time to time, a few inquirers; but the appalling confession forced to the lips even then is, "The children are come to the birth, and there is not strength to bring forth."

And now, brethren, what shall be done? We must go back to the point of departure. When Bunyan's Christian got out of the way and found himself in sore trouble, his burden growing heavier instead of lighter, Evangelist told him he must go back, and enter the path to the wicket-gate, where he left it. "Then did Christian address himself to go back."

And then what? How shall we prevent a repetition of this turning aside and turning back from the narrow way? We must have the love of God as the supreme and masterful affection of our soul. The love of the world must be eradicated from the heart. And this can be done only by enthroning a new spiritual affection. Chalmers's phrase, set as the title of a sermon, "The expulsive power of a new affection," contains the whole philosophy of a holy, devout Christian life.

We must know this "power" in a conscious daily experience. To love God according to His character and worth is to subdue and extirpate every other affection. Then the Christian's course will be onward and upward, like the sun, and no more steps backward, and no more aside.

> "As by the light of opening day
> The stars are all concealed;
> So earthly pleasures fade away
> When Jesus is revealed."

" Love not the world, neither the things of the world. If any man love the world, the love of the Father is not in him."

No. 4. *Published by direction of the Congregational Churches of Boston.*

THE
DUTY OF CHRISTIANS

TO UNITE WITH SOME CHURCH;

AND THE

DUTY OF CHURCH MEMBERS

TO UNITE WITH THE CHURCH WHERE THEY STATEDLY WORSHIP.

By REV. S. P. FAY.

BOSTON:
NICHOLS AND NOYES.
1866.

THE

DUTY OF CHRISTIANS

TO UNITE WITH SOME CHURCH;

AND THE

DUTY OF CHURCH MEMBERS

TO UNITE WITH THE CHURCH WHERE THEY STATEDLY WORSHIP.

By REV. S. P. FAY.

BOSTON:
NICHOLS AND NOYES.
1866.

Entered according to Act of Congress, in the year 1866, by

NICHOLS AND NOYES,

In the Clerk's Office of the District Court of the District of Massachusetts.

CAMBRIDGE:
STEREOTYPED AND PRINTED BY JOHN WILSON AND SONS.

The Duty of Christians and Church Members.

WE are told, in Acts iv. 23, that, as soon as Peter and John had been dismissed by the chief priests, " they went to their own company," they went to their old friends, and returned to their Church-fellowship. They neither thought themselves exalted above their brethren, nor were they deterred from joining their own company, either by their desire of ease or by the fear of the wrath of their rulers. If they had followed their own personal wishes, they might have retired to their closets, and spent their time in quiet, peaceful retirement; but they were men in a public station, and must seek the public good also. They knew that their place was with their own company; and, in going " to their own company," they revealed a law of our nature. It is this, that we associate with those of our own kind. We choose our social circle; we choose our party. We unite ourselves with those who are most like ourselves. We may not be able to agree with them in all points, to indorse every thing that the majority receive; but we go with those in politics and social life, that, in most particulars, are of our " own company." Much more in religious matters, " being let go " from the bondage of sin, should we " go to our own company."

I wish to apply this principle to those who think they have accepted the plan of salvation by Jesus Christ, and are seeking to lead lives of secret devotion, but who have made no public choice of the side on which they stand. They think they have accepted Christ as their Saviour, but do not join themselves with His followers. They seek to serve Christ in secret, but leave the Christian community utterly in doubt to which party they belong. They hope that they are Christians; but, if they are, they refuse " to go to their own company."

Now, I maintain, and wish to illustrate and enforce the principle, — first, that it is the duty of every Christian to unite with some Church; and, secondly, that it is his duty to unite with the Church where he statedly worships.

In the New Testament, we find the Church referred to under two ideas. (1.) The Church as the aggregate of *true believers*. This includes all those who have been redeemed by Christ, and of which Christ is the spiritual Head: all who are regenerated by the Holy Ghost, and only such, belong to this Church, universal and invisible. It is the assembly of believers, and it is evident that only believers do in fact belong to it. Others may profess to do so, and the genuineness of their profession may not be suspected; but the revelations of the last day will discover the mistake, and show that they never were members of the true Church, however they might be called by the name of Christ. The only means of access into this Church is regeneration by the Spirit of God. "He that climbeth up some other way is a thief and a robber."

But, (2) besides this spiritual body, there is the Church as an association of professed disciples,—an organized, localized, officered body, into which are to be gathered all those who are *supposed* to be the true disciples of Christ. Such was the " Church of God which was at Corinth," " the Church of Laodicea," each of " the seven Churches of Asia." When Christ gave to His followers a rule of discipline for His Church, in Matt. xviii. 15–18, they understood that all believers, who in their totality would constitute the one enduring Church, would also enter into forms of association, under mutual obligations and responsibilities. I have not space to develop the idea at length, and can only say that the truth is abundantly and clearly established in the New Testament, that Christ meant that all such as profess to be real saints, and appear to be so in the eye of Christian charity, should be gathered into and constitute a gospel Church. This is meant by the Church when Christ says to Peter, " Upon this rock will I build my Church; and the gates of hell shall not prevail against it." The idea is fundamental that this visible Church is not a voluntary and human association. It is a distinct and entirely different society and kingdom from civil, worldly associations and confederations: it is of Divine authority. It is called, in the Scriptures, " the kingdom of heaven," " the kingdom of God and of Christ," Who said,

"My kingdom is not of this world." Christ is the Founder and Head of the Church. He "loved the Church and gave Himself for it, that He might present it to Himself a glorious Church, not having spot or wrinkle, or any such thing," and " God hath put all things under His feet, and gave Him to be the Head over all things to the Church." If, now, the visible Church is of Divine authority, and is organized by the command, and according to the rules, of Christ, for the perfecting of His saints and the observance of His ordinances, then it follows that the disciples of Christ are not at liberty to belong to it or not. They are bound, by every relationship to Christ, to belong to it. But there are special reasons why all who have been regenerated by the Holy Ghost will naturally go to their own company, the Church.

1. A very obvious and conclusive reason is, because the Saviour commands it. Simple, prompt obedience to all of God's commands is the chief characteristic of every true child. It is hard to see where one can get the evidence of adoption without obedience. The Bible does not leave you at liberty to follow your inclinations

or caprices. You are bound to obey the commands of the Master at all hazards. Christ says, "If ye love Me, ye will keep My commandments." Now, the command is most plain and positive: "Take, eat; this is My body broken for you." This was a general command, given to all disciples, because the sacrament itself was designed for all disciples. If you are a disciple, the command is addressed to you. Put, now, this command with that other strong statement of our Saviour, "Whosoever, therefore, shall confess Me before men, him will I confess before My Father Which is in heaven; but whosoever shall deny Me before men, him will I also deny before My Father Which is in heaven." The expression, "before men," shows the act here referred to, to be a public one. It is a clear declaration, that, if we refuse to obey the Divine command to confess Christ before men, Christ will deny before His Father that we are His disciples. This is in exact agreement with the principle laid down in 2 Cor., chap. vi., respecting separation from the world; and the conclusion of the apostle is, "Wherefore come out from among them, and be ye separate, saith the Lord." Do you say, " I am not good enough to eat of the bread and drink of the cup"? But God knew just how bad you were, when He commanded you to "eat." He knew what even the wife of your bosom did not know. If you are a disciple, He commands you to come to His table, and He assures you that His blood shall cleanse from all stain and spot. He says, "Come; because I live, you shall live also."

But you ask, "If I join the Church, shall I not bring dishonor upon it? If I make a profession of religion, shall I not make matters worse for the side I pretend to take? If I knew I could live a consistent religious life, I would make a profession; but I do not wish to lead a life that would dishonor Christ." But what are you *now* doing but dishonoring Christ? Is the obligation to obey Christ on those in the Church more than on those out of the Church? Is not every disciple a child of God, and under one law? A man that stays away from duty and from God dishonors the cause of God, whether he is in the Church or out of it. You cannot bring half as much dishonor upon the cause of Christ by trying to obey Him, as you do now while you publicly refuse to obey the command to eat and drink "in remembrance" of Christ.

2. Christ has not only commanded us to eat and drink, but He has enjoined it upon us under the most impressive conditions. "This do in remembrance of Me." It was His dying command; this fact ought to bind us to obedience. "He died for us, that they which live should not henceforth live unto themselves, but unto Him Who died for them and rose again." Look at the facts. You were dead in sinfulness, in guilt, under the law. God was against you, a holy God, and you unholy. You were proud, prayerless, and ungodly. But Christ came and died, that you might live: He spoke to you in love. That love was the procuring cause of all your mercies here and hopes hereafter. He established the Church, and instituted the sacrament on purpose to commemorate that wondrous love; and, with His dying lips, He asks you to eat and drink in remembrance of Him. Can any *Christian* heart refuse to obey the command? Will not the love of Christ constrain you to do this act in remembrance of Him? This is one of the first things that a man should do, when God has delivered him from the bondage of sin and the power of the Devil. It is the least that he can

do. Nobody else has suffered so much on his account as Christ; nobody else has such a claim upon his remembrance. When Christ has accepted him, and promised to save him, and healed his lusts and his appetites, there is nothing more rational and right than that he should stand up and take the vows of Christ upon him. Under such circumstances, silence and hiding God's work in the soul is monstrously ungrateful and wicked. And therefore, when Christ says, " Do this in remembrance of me," He commands you to do that which accords with every sentiment of gratitude, and with every sense of justice.

3. It is a testimony to the Divine cause, to God's law and Christ's kingdom in this world, that you are in duty bound to give.

There are two opposing forces in this world, and there is no third party: God and mammon, righteousness and sin, the Church and the world, — these are drawn up in sharp and bitter warfare. Our Master declared that this world was the battle-field on which God and Satan were in conflict; and He says, " He that is not with me is against me." The conflict is still going on unabated in your day and mine. We are born into a world where struggle and strife are the law of moral growth. We are born into a world where two great contending influences — right and wrong — are seeking to overthrow each other; and the conflict will go on. You can take your choice as to which side you will be arrayed upon. You *cannot* take your choice as to whether you will be arrayed upon either or not. There is no middle ground. You are not at liberty, in this matter, to be indifferent. Under the circumstances in which you are placed, indifference is a sin. When the eternal welfare of your own friends and children is involved in your example, indifference is a crime. You are bound to determine which side you will take. God established the Church, that he might gather into it all who are His friends. He says to every man, "Choose you this day whom you will serve." Oh, how many there are in these congregations, who have been standing for a long while, feeling that they ought to be Christians, and that they ought to let it be known that they are Christians! but they have been ashamed of the service of Christ, they have been ashamed of themselves. They have been standing irresolute and uncommitted. They have not represented Christ before men. Whatsoever good things they may have had in the family, they have hid their light "under a bushel." Men do not think they are Christians, even though they may be; and it is time that you came out, and acknowledged your allegiance to Christ. It is time that the sanctuary became a safe place; for you are in danger of wearing out your heart and conscience. You are in danger of wearing out your susceptibility to truths that are most sacred. Woe be to you, if you have no taste for the bread or water of life, or for the fruit of the tree of life! Woe be to him who has lost conscience and faith and love and aspiration! and, under the circumstances in which God has placed you, you cannot help losing all these and more, by your continued refusal to give this public testimony to the Divine cause. The sense of gratitude must compel you to this course. You are the perpetual recipient of God's mercies. Christ has redeemed you from sin. There is not one moment in which He does not brood over you with His thoughts of love. And by what public act on your part has there been manifested any love or gratitude or recognition, that answered to the noble affection which He has displayed towards you? I do not ask you whether you believe in this Church or that, whether you hold to this doctrine or that: I present to you this love of God that has upheld you all the days of your life, and then lay before you the command of Christ, "Do this in remembrance of me," and ask you this question: Can you, with reason, with honor, with gratitude, with any sentiment that man ought to cherish, be indifferent to it? Can you refuse this act of public recognition of the love of God towards you?

But I must pass now to speak of "the duty of Church members to unite with the Church where they statedly worship."

Instability is one of the marked characteristics of our times. Men change their opinions and their pursuits, their residences and their connections, political, social, and religious, almost as easily as they change their dress. Hence the counsel of the Apostle, to be "steadfast, immovable," has gone into disrepute, so that the Christian world "abounds" less than it ought "in the work of the Lord."

Multitudes of Christians, in " good and regular standing," move their residence, but leave their covenant vows and Church relations at home. They give two reasons for doing so: 1. Because they love the Church of their first espousal to Christ so much that they cannot endure to take their names from it. But if you have taken your personal presence and services from it, if your personal influence cannot be given to it, of what value is your name to it? It can only go to swell the list of those, who, being away from the watch and care of the Church, in scenes and temptations unknown to it, are a source of constant anxiety to every faithful Church. Nothing gives a Church, that is true to its Covenant vows, so much anxiety as its column of " absentees." Hence, a true and right love for the Church would constrain you to take your name from that list, if, in the providence of God, you are compelled to forsake it, in regard to your bodily presence and personal helpfulness.

Because they are uncertain how long they shall remain in a given place. But, if you remain long enough to take the trouble to move your goods, your residence, your family, you surely can take the trouble to remove your Church relationship, which can be done simply for the asking. This were better if you were to remove every six months. Your letter will be your introduction into the new Christian community. It will give you a spiritual *home* while you stay. And the re-examination as to your faith, and the reasons for your hope, and the reconsecration of yourself to the new Church, will tend to make you a live Christian.

I think there is something in the column of " absent," as given by the statistical Secretary in the " Congregational Quarterly," to make our Churches sad. This column is imperfect, because many Churches do not give their " absentees."

In Massachusetts, nineteen Churches reporting 4,172 members do not give the number of " absentees." Deducting this from the total, and you find 71,246, of whom 11,706 are absentees; *i.e.*, one-sixth of the whole are absentees. Our own Churches in this city report (Mariner's Church not counted) 4,960 members. Of these, the Old South and Central Church, with a membership of 718 do not give the number of " absentees;" deducting these two Churches, and out of a membership of 4,242 we find 889 absentees. Where are these absent ones? Who is watching over them, and seeking their edification as we covenanted to do? Are they guilty of a breach of covenant in withdrawing "from the watch and communion of the saints"? But other Churches send their members to us also. Let any Church in our city make an accurate estimate of the number of Church members elsewhere, who are worshipping with it without taking letters to it, and the result will be most significant. One who was a pastor in one of our neighboring Churches, searched this matter out carefully, and found this class forty per cent of the whole number belonging to his Church. It is to be feared that this case is not an exceptional one. There is something wrong here. There is a defect somewhere. Either Churches are unfaithful to their covenant vows, or there is a sad depreciation of this solemn value of covenant vows on the part of the absent themselves.

The evil of this whole matter is, that it is a *practical* disowning of the Church relation. It is true, in theory, that these can never "be as they have been." The solemn vows "go with them through life and accompany them to the bar of God." They are everywhere and always accountable to God for the manner in which they keep these vows. But they are vows made to be kept in connection with the visible Church. Yet the Church at home cannot watch over them, and they cannot labor in connection with it, and they refuse to unite themselves with the people of God where they are. Are they not practically removed from the watch and care of the Church? There is something in our very nature which forces us to feel less perfectly an obligation which we do not *acknowledge* with those with whom we worship. Our vows do not bind us so perfectly, because we have not renewed our promise to keep them where God has cast our lot.

Then, also, it brings upon us the weakness of a divided heart. The vows of the professed follower of Christ bind him to give his affections and energies to the Church where his name is recorded. But his bodily presence and his daily interests bind him to the Church where he worships; and so, by a law of our nature, in this divided state of his heart his labors are paralyzed. His sympathy cannot flow forth strongly; and so, by a natural consequence, he becomes absorbed in pleasures, or in the acquisition of honor, or in the accumulation of wealth. No man will labor with all his heart for the Master where he resides, unless the covenant vows of God are upon him. This is why God requires us to become His by taking upon ourselves the obligation, and pronouncing the voluntary pledge, the recorded and blood-sealed oath. In going from the familiar home of his early consecration, the Christian needs to carry his armor with him, and put it on, and openly range himself shoulder to shoulder with the followers of Christ. He must unite himself with the people of God where he is, and make to himself a new home for his faith, and a new field for his Christian service. The exigencies of no man's condition can be met by a hidden and secret Christian life, or by an occasional, incidental, and easy effort, or by worshipping here to-day and there to-morrow. That is not complying with the exhortation of Christ to " strive to enter in at the strait gate." The gate was designed expressly for entering; and God desires that men shall enter, and has established His Church, and made arrangements for all to enter, and He says, "strive, *agonize* to enter in," *i.e.*, put forth every effort. When the mild and calm Saviour speaks thus, I know that there is peril about; I know that there is danger which may well arrest the attention and call out the utmost skill and exertion of man. No Church, no Christian man, can afford to be indifferent in regard to these covenant vows. In the midst of peril and the thunder of excitement in a city like this, that man is especially in danger who is least awake. No man can afford to live without taking these covenant vows fully upon himself. No man can afford to treat the question of his soul's welfare as you do who make no profession, or you who think you can live and prosper without carrying the covenant vows with you wherever you go. You are drifting on towards the ocean of eternity with the idea, perhaps, that you are about as well off as other people. You look about you, and see a great many people who are living as you do, while they hope they are Christians, and perhaps have recorded their vows some hundreds of miles away; and you say, "I am as good as they are, and, if they go to heaven, I shall." But suppose that neither of you are going there. Our Lord declares that there are many who will go up in the last day, and say, " Lord, Lord, have we not prophesied in Thy name, and in Thy name cast out devils, and in Thy name done many wonderful works?" and who will hear the response, " I never knew you." All the probabilities certainly are that this number will be largely taken from those who have never confessed Christ before men, or, having confessed Him, are living in careless neglect of their Church relations. By all the honor that is in you, by all the truth that is in you, by the hope of your soul's health and happiness, I beseech of you to flee within the sacred enclosure of the Church. "Take unto you the whole armor of God, that ye may be able to withstand in the evil day, and, having done all, to stand."

No. 5. *Published by direction of the Congregational Churches of Boston.*

THE DUTY

OF

DAILY SECRET PRAYER

AND

DAILY STUDY OF THE BIBLE.

BY

Rev. J. M. MANNING.

BOSTON:
NICHOLS AND NOYES.
1866.

THE DUTY

OF

DAILY SECRET PRAYER

AND

DAILY STUDY OF THE BIBLE.

BY

Rev. J. M. MANNING.

BOSTON:
NICHOLS AND NOYES.
1866.

Entered according to Act of Congress, in the year 1866, by

NICHOLS AND NOYES,

In the Clerk's Office of the District Court of the District of Massachusetts.

CAMBRIDGE:
STEREOTYPED AND PRINTED BY JOHN WILSON AND SONS.

ALONE WITH GOD.

A TIME comes, in the experience of every true Christian, when the words, "enter into thy closet," are no more the stern command which they once were, but one of the sweetest of all Christ's invitations. The moments set apart for our secret devotions are "the children's hour" in the Divine family. You know how it is wont to be in the household where love reigns. The child grows weary of playing, and steals away to the door of the room in which the father is. It finds that door ajar, and hears, from within, a voice of welcome. And so, entering in and having shut the door, it climbs upon the father's knees, is folded in his arms, and hangs about his neck, interchanging kisses of affection with him, and hearing tender replies to all its little story of wants and troubles, till its heart is made to overflow with comfort and gladness.

And is it at all otherwise, only unspeakably more blessed, with the soul which has learned to turn toward God, and say, "Abba, Father"? That new-born soul is forced to pass much of its time in a temporal world, where it finds many disturbances. It is driven hither and thither by unholy impulses. It is tossed up and down upon a sea of temptations. It is deceived, misled, betrayed, disappointed, until it cries out, as did the poor Prodigal, for its Father. And that Father, "Who seeth in secret," hears the cry of the distressed child. He is near it, in the calm and retired place, saying, "Enter in, thou bewildered and helpless one, and rest thee for an hour, communing with Me. Has the storm dealt hardly with thy little bark? Here, in 'thy closet,' is its haven of peaceful waters. Have the archers shot at thee, and art thou sorely wounded? Here, in 'thy closet,' is the balm of Gilead. Thy spirit hungers for food which the world cannot give: here it is, 'the bread of heaven,' of which if a man eat, he shall never hunger. Poor child of immortality, thou art thirsty; and here is 'the water of life,' which, if thou drink it, shall be in thee a well of water springing up into everlasting life. Come, thou weary child, born of Mine own Spirit, and refresh thee in thy Father's love! 'Enter into thy closet,' and be alone with Me in that secret place, until thou shalt learn how much more ready than any earthly parent I am to give good gifts unto My children." Such, though alas! how unworthily spoken by my poor lips, is the mind of the Father towards us, when He bids us enter into our closet, and shut the door, and pray in secret to Him.

This meeting with the Father in secret, in order to fulfil its blessed purpose, must be distinguished by three things,— the reading of the Scriptures, self-examination, prayer. These may be considered separately, though, in experience, each of them involves the other two. You cannot examine yourself in the light of God, without praying all the time, "Create in me a clean heart, and renew a right spirit within me." Together with your reading of the Scriptures goes forward that process of your own thoughts, "accusing, or else excusing, one another." And even while you pray, uttering the weakness and longings of which you are conscious, you find no words but those of the Spirit adequate to your groanings. As a vessel escapes from the tempest into its quiet harbor by means of three things, — ballast to keep it low in the water, sails to catch the wind, and a helm to guide its course, — so the Christian returns into his rest in the closet by means of self-examination, prayer, and reading of the Scriptures, all helping together. It is the Scriptures, read with a docile spirit, that hold him to his course; it is beholding himself in the light of God that keeps him low in his own thoughts; it is crying, "Abba, Father," that bears him consciously on into his rest. Each of these exercises so involves the others, that, if you are diligent in either of them, you will be in all; and, if you neglect either one, you will become negligent of them all. As soon as you begin to examine yourself, you will look for the perfect standard with which to compare your life and character. As soon as you begin to know that standard, you will begin to cry, "God be merciful to me a sinner." If you tell me that you never pray, then I know that you are not a faithful student of the Bible and your own heart. If I could persuade you to attend to either of these duties as you should, I might feel sure that you would soon be attending to them all.

And what words of persuasion shall I speak?— But hold a moment, fellow-disciple, and consider what I am proposing to do. Persuade you, who profess to be God's child, to have a time and place for meeting with that Father! Can it be that any such persuasion is needed? Oh, where is my charity! do I not, with cruel tongue, speak evil against you falsely, when I intimate that you have not daily communings with God, in your closet? Persuading you, at this late day, to do that in which the new life begins, and which is its light of life for evermore! The conversion of the apostle Paul was proved by his praying. The Lord said to His servant Ananias, "Arise, and go into the street which is called Straight, and inquire in the house of Judas for one called Saul, of Tarsus; for, behold, he prayeth." Ananias need be afraid of him no longer. He had been born into God's family: God had begotten him, through the Spirit, to be a dear child; and the voice of that sonship in him was a prayer, feebly lisped in the dawn of the truth that God was his Father, and to be spoken more articulately, and with a richer fulness, as he grew toward the stature of a man in Christ Jesus. A prayerless Christian! that seems impossible. To be a Christian is to partake of the life of Christ. But the life of Christ was that of a Divine sonship in humanity. That sonship was a being in the Father as His dear child, knowing Him, and being known of Him, as in this tender fellowship, — a fellowship which was expressed by the Son in prayer, and by the Father in hearing and answering that prayer. So, if you pray not, as Christ did, what can we say but that you have no part in Him? Can you be God's child if you never call on Him as your Father? if, when you hear Him say, "Seek My face," you answer not, "Lord, Thy face will I seek"? If you have been born of the free woman, how is it that you speak not the language of the free woman? Should not the children of Canaan use the speech of Canaan?

Let God decide the question. I see not how it can be, yet will assume as true what a Council of Pastors and Delegates, representing five thousand Church-members, has said of the prayerlessness of Christians. It may, in some mysterious manner, be true, that you are a child of God, though you have not the power to call Him Father. The Holy Spirit, let us assume, may have begotten you from the dead, and made you a partaker of Christ's life, though you are not conscious of such a life, " hid with Christ in God." Granting that this life of sonship is in you, though so stupefied by worldliness as to have no longing unto the Father, no filial impulse to go and meet that Father in the secrecy of the closet; how, then, shall you be persuaded to make that closet your daily resort, till the heart of the child in you shall find its voice in finding the heart of the Father?

First, think upon the life of Christ, and how large a space in that life was filled by His secret communion with God. He prayed so much, and entered so fully into the mind of the Father, as to seem almost to carry His closet about with Him wherever He went. Appearing outwardly to men, in temporal form and vesture, He yet inhabited eternity,—dwelt " in the bosom of the Father."

This spiritual indwelling was that which most filled His consciousness; so that, even in the midst of earthly disturbances, He could at any moment make Himself alone with God. We read of Him as absorbed in works of love; yet, even while performing those works, rejoicing in spirit, and saying, "I thank Thee, O Father, Lord of heaven and earth:" saying these words in such a way as to indicate that nothing temporal, but only the eternal, was in His thoughts, — no consciousness of any thing but a being in the Father, Who was also in Him. So at the grave of Lazarus, while touched with the sorrow of Mary and Martha, and while the company of Jews present were angrily watching Him, this whole scene being shut out from the sanctuary of His spirit, "He lifted up His eyes, and said, Father, I thank Thee that Thou hast heard Me; and I knew that Thou hearest Me always." This was to Him a praying in secret, and His prayer was answered openly in the coming forth of His friend from the grave. In like manner, when He prayed for His disciples at the Last Supper, all His words came out of eternity and the Father's bosom. Nothing earthly or temporal disturbs Him. He is conscious only of being in the high sphere and region of His own divinity, as a beloved Son communing with the infinite Father, praying in the secrecy of His spirit.

Yet even Christ, thus always in secret with the Father, had His hours for going away by Himself and praying. We read of Him in a certain place, that " He was alone praying." The whole tenor of His life, as sketched by Luke, was this: " In the day-time He was teaching in the temple; and at night He went out, and abode in the mount that is called the Mount of Olives." When He came to His disciples in the fourth watch of the night, walking to their drowning ship on the boiling waves, they knew that He came out of His place of prayer, where He had been " abiding under the shadow of the Almighty." — " And it came to pass in those days," says one of the Evangelists, " that He went out into a mountain to pray, and continued all night in prayer." After His baptism, being consecrated to His redeeming work by the coming of the Spirit upon Him, He went away into the wilderness, and was there forty days and forty nights alone with the beasts of the earth. Oh, how those long hours of communion with God strengthened Him to vanquish the Tempter, to hold fast His faith that He was the Son of God; to undertake for lost men, who, as He foresaw, would lay on Him the burden of their hatred and scorn, and nail Him in their wrath to the shameful cross! And when He saw that cross prepared, waiting that He might be lifted up upon it, He went over the brook into a place where was a garden; and there, curtained by the night and the shadows of the olive-trees, He girded himself for the sacrifice. "Being in an agony, He prayed." And then He came to His disciples, and found them sleeping; whereupon He went away again and prayed; and then again the third time, in the very same words; until at last He overcame His great sorrow, found Himself able to drink the cup which might not pass from Him, could respond perfectly to the judgment of the Father against sin, saying, "Thy will, not Mine, be done!"

Now, if the holy Son of God, who was without sin or sinful taint, and Who dwelt in the bosom of the Father, was wont thus to feed the sources of His spiritual life by setting apart hours for drawing near to God in prayer, how should we do, who are by nature strangers, the children of God only by a second birth, but feebly conscious as yet of the new life in us, and prone to evil? If He needed that strengthening which comes by abiding in the Father, then we should not dare trust ourselves a day, no, nor an hour, without it. He is not ashamed to call us brethren, though so little of His consciousness of sonship is in us. That consciousness was so vivid and constant in Him as to enable Him, amid scenes of the greatest confusion, to call God "Father." But we, even in the still hour of meditation, can hardly lisp the infant's cry, "Abba, Father." Oh, then, if we would meet the brotherliness which is in Christ, and, together with Him, would have our life hid in God, calling God "Father" with the full and articulate voice of our spirits, must we not again and again, and often and regularly, with the outgoings of the morning and evening, and "in season and out of season," enter into our closet, and shut the door, and pray to our Father who seeth in secret?

Turning now from Christ to those who have most nearly resembled Him in being the children of God, we shall find that in the closet was the hiding of their power. "Enoch walked with God." And this life of prayer, which he lived in a wicked age, gave him power to be translated, that he should not see death. Abraham had so much of this spirit, and communed with the Lord so often in secret places, that he was called "the friend of God." Jacob was named Israel, because he wrestled in prayer till he prevailed. When Moses came down out of the mount, his face shone so that the people were afraid to meet him; and that shining, so dreadful to consciences defiled by idolatry, was but the outward glow of a soul irradiated by the light of God, and filled and suffused with almighty power by being so long in the companionship of Jehovah. Such was the empowering of which Samuel, and Elijah, and Daniel, and Isaiah, and even Jeremiah, were conscious by entering into prayer before God. Herein was their inspiration; this the live coal, from off the altar, which touched their lips. Take out of the record of those holy men of old the accounts we have of their secret prayers and longings unto God, and the charm of that record would be gone. The little remnant of outward fact would be dull and stale. You can no more think of those men without tracing all their wondrous words and works to the fountain of communion with God, than you can think of a river as possible without a source, or of the light of day as existing without a sun. Whom did God make ruler of His people, so that the kings of the earth feared him, and call "a man after His own heart," but David? — David, full of evil impulses, yet who loved to "draw nigh to God;" whose sweet Psalms, the joy of all burdened hearts, are but the voice of his own heart praying in secret; who called upon the Lord in the morning, at evening, and during the night-watches; who envied the bird that had her nest in the wall of the house of prayer; whose "heart panted after God," and "cried out for the living God;" who was constantly exclaiming, "When shall I come, and appear before God?" How almost sadly we read, "The prayers of David, the son of Jesse, are ended," feeling that then his life must have ended; or, if he lived after he had ceased to pray, that he must have been a weak and miserable old man, all the sweet freshness and strength of his early manhood having gone from him!

The words "human strength" seem at times to have no meaning. All our strength is weakness, and "power belongeth unto God;" and it is in His strength only that we feel ourselves to be really strong. And it is our prayer, the voice of the child in us longing unto its Father, that makes us conscious of receiving God's strength, even as the branch receives the life of the vine, by abiding in it. There is nothing men desire so much as the consciousness of power. This explains their indecent "haste to be rich," and scramblings for office or for the magic of a great name. But no such consciousness of power comes by these means, as comes to the Christian when he feels himself empowered from on high. This is the power of God in his soul, — a spiritual might, by which he can do all things, subduing his own evil nature, "overcoming the world," "bearing all things, hoping all things, believing all things, enduring all things." — "In us, that is, in our flesh, dwelleth no good thing;" nor have we any power of ourselves, either to do or think any thing as we ought, save as God works in us, "both to will and to do of His good pleasure." And this inworking comes through prayer, being that "secret of the Lord" which is "with them that fear Him." And oh, what pleasure they have with whom this secret ever abides! I have no doubt that we here lay open the source of all that is greatest, purest, and best of man's doing. Out of this dwelling in God as a dear child, came the "Confessions" of Augustine, the sermons of Massillon, the "Thoughts" of Pascal, the conceptions of Michael Angelo, the sustained fervor of Whitfield. The singing men and singing women, whose hymns make melody in the Churches all round the world, have caught their inspiration in that secret fellowship of God into which prayer is the appointed way. We understand the patriotism of Washington, the missionary zeal of Brainerd, the courage of Luther, and the patience of the great company of saints "of whom the world was not worthy," by knowing that they went often, and were always going, into secret places of prayer; where the spirit of the child in them uttered itself beseechingly, till they felt the life of the Father raising them up into "newness of life," and His Spirit witnessing with theirs that they were born of Him.

Let it be distinctly noticed that Christ, **and**

those His brethren who have most largely shared in His experience of sonship, have never felt any embarrassment in coming before God to pray, — as though their asking were a doubting of the Divine goodness, or a putting of their private wish in the way of changeless decrees. If God were a law of nature, or a fate, we might feel an impropriety in prayer. But He is our Father; and He is ready to do for us above all that we are able to ask, or even to think; and, when we are brought into perfect accord with Him in the way of childlike prayer, only then do we grasp the truth of this exceeding readiness to bless; and in this knowing of God as our unwithholding Father is that "eternal life" which is both the hearing and answering of prayer, and to which there need be added no other granting of our requests. "Do you pray as a child of God, whose first and nearest relationship is to God, your Father; whose most deeply felt interests are bound up in that relation, in what lies within the circle of that relation contemplated in itself? Do you pray as one to whom the mind of God towards you and your own mind towards Him are the most important elements of existence, and whose other interests in existence are as outer circles around this central interest; so that you see yourself, and your family, and your friends, and your country, and your race, with the eyes, because with the heart, of one who 'loves the Lord his God with all his heart and mind and soul and strength'? Is this at least your ideal for yourself; what you are seeking to realize,—to realize for its own sake, not for any consequences of it in time or eternity? for, whatever the blessed consequences of its realization will be, they shall be far, and for ever inferior and secondary to itself." *

But perhaps you plead that I have, in these remarks, transcended any thing you have ever experienced of the rewards of secret prayer. You have many times consecrated a closet, but have always forsaken it after a brief trial; for you found no upliftings of soul, no inspirations, no enlargings of your joy and strength, such as I have described. Let us see, then, if the causes of your discouragement cannot be laid open; and if you cannot be put in such a way of performing this duty as never again to neglect it, but, on the contrary, to esteem it the one pleasure of your

* John McLeod Campbell.

life, with which you shall allow no engagements or stress of worldly business to interfere.

Your closet is a dreary and barren place for just this: you do not, as God's child, so experience daily your own weakness as to feel driven to your Father for strength. And why is not this experience of weakness constantly yours? Because your new life is not a conflict with the powers of darkness, with which you are unable to cope, save in the strength of God. It is the consciousness that the battle is going against him, that causes the child of God to take refuge in his "Strong Tower." Oh blessed danger, that forces us to fly into our "Fortress," where we find the peace which passeth understanding! If you, compassed about with infirmities, are daily striving to live the life of the holy Son of God, then are you in a conflict which is continually forcing from you the prayer, "Father, save me from this hour." Are you not driven every day to the utterance of such "strong crying with tears"? Then you cannot be struggling to put down all your evil thoughts, to overcome the world, to convert sinners from the error of their ways, and to bear about the dying and the life of Christ daily in your mortal body. The sons of God do perpetually experience that they are utterly weak, powerless to be in perfect accord with the mind of the Father. Billows go over their head, and they are all the time ready to perish. Not allowing themselves to be drifted along in the currents of worldliness, but being in the way of their holy purpose to be conformed to God, they have such experience of weakness as to be ever crying, "Father, Abba Father, keep us through Thine own name, for we are Thy children; calm us, strengthen us, lead us, give us the victory over foes too mighty for our strength." And, finding that prayer answered, — daily answered in their closet, where they pray to the Father in secret, — answered with such consciousness of deliverance, and of incomings of peace, joy, and strength, — the bitterest deprivation of their life would be not to be allowed to pray, while in praying they receive a thousand-fold for all their conflicts and troubles.

"Father, I'm now alone with Thee!
Thy voice to hear, Thy face to see,
And feel Thy presence near;
It is not Fancy's lovely dream,
Though wondrous e'en to Faith it seem,
That Thou dost wait me here.

A moment from this outward life,
Its service, self-denial, strife,
   I joyfully retreat;
My soul, through intercourse with Thee,
Strengthened, refreshed, and calmed shall be,
   Its scenes again to meet.

How sweet, how solemn, thus to lie,
And feel Jehovah's searching eye
   On me well pleased can rest!
Because with His beloved Son
The Father's grace has made me one,
   I must be always blest.

The secret pangs I could not tell
To dearest friend, Thou knowest well;
   They claim Thy gracious heart;
Thou dost remove with tender care,
Or sweetly give me strength to bear
   The sanctifying smart.

Thy presence has a wondrous power!
The sharpest thorn becomes a flower,
   And breathes a sweet perfume;
Whate'er looked dark and sad before
With happy light shines silvered o'er;
   There's no such thing as gloom!"

Addresses to Church Members

BY THE

CONGREGATIONAL PASTORS OF BOSTON,

RECOMMENDED BY THE

Boston Congregational Council.

The following are now published, and ready for delivery:—

No. 1. THE RESULT OF COUNCIL. Complete.

No. 2. THE CHRISTIAN'S RECONSECRATION. By Rev. E. K. ALDEN, Pastor of Phillips Church.

No. 3. THE WORLDLINESS OF NOMINAL CHRISTIANS. By Rev. Dr. WEBB, Pastor of Shawmut Church.

No. 4. THE DUTY OF CHRISTIANS TO UNITE WITH SOME CHURCH, AND THE DUTY OF CHURCH-MEMBERS TO UNITE WITH THE CHURCH WHERE THEY STATEDLY WORSHIP. By Rev. S. P. FAY, Pastor of Salem Church.

THE DUTY OF DAILY SECRET PRAYER and DAILY STUDY OF THE BIBLE. By Rev. J. M. MANNING.

The remaining Addresses will follow at intervals of about one week; viz:—

REVIVALS OF RELIGION. By Rev. J. E. TODD.

THE SPREAD OF THE GOSPEL IN THE CITY AMONG THE POOR, AND THOSE WHO HABITUALLY NEGLECT THE SERVICES OF THE SABBATH. By Rev. Dr. DEXTER.

THE CHRISTIAN'S DUTY TO WORK FOR THE SAVING OF SOULS. By Rev. Mr. BINGHAM.

THE DUTY OF A MORE STRICT OBSERVANCE OF THE SABBATH. By Rev. Dr. BLAGDEN.

THE POWER AND OFFICE OF THE HOLY SPIRIT. By Rev. Dr. ADAMS.

THE POWER OF PRAYER. By Rev. Dr. KIRK.

THE DIVINE SOVEREIGNTY IN ITS RELATION TO HUMAN SALVATION. By Rev. Mr. BAKER.

No. 6. Published by direction of the Congregational Churches of Boston.

REVIVALS OF RELIGION.

BY

Rev. J. E. TODD.

BOSTON:
NICHOLS AND NOYES.
1866.

REVIVALS OF RELIGION.

BY

Rev. J. E. TODD.

BOSTON:
NICHOLS AND NOYES.
1866.

Entered according to Act of Congress, in the year 1866, by

NICHOLS AND NOYES,

In the Clerk's Office of the District Court of the District of Massachusetts.

CAMBRIDGE:
STEREOTYPED AND PRINTED BY JOHN WILSON AND SONS.

REVIVALS OF RELIGION.

Are revivals desirable?

IT is too late to discuss this question. As well might we discuss the desirableness of summer showers. It is evident that they are a part, and a blessed part, of the Divine administration. It may be said that religious interest ought to be continual rather than fitful; that it would be better for a Church to be perpetually alive, rather than occasionally revived. But an occasional increase of interest does not necessitate a low state of religion at ordinary times. And the question is, not what might be, but what, in the present imperfect state of sanctified human nature and under the present dispensation of the Spirit, is possible. From the day of Pentecost until now, the growth, and even the existence, of the Church has been largely owing to revivals. Whatever of life and earnestness there is in any of our Churches has originated in and been fed by revivals. Most of those who have been redeemed from off the face of the earth were converted in revivals: almost every faithful minister of the Gospel and missionary has traced his conversion to a revival. And the hope of the Church for the future is in revivals. If ever the kingdoms of this world are to become the kingdom of our Lord; if ever the Church of Christ is to be redeemed from schism, heresy, and worldliness, and made pure, earnest, and living; if ever our impenitent friends are to be brought to Christ; if ever we ourselves are to make the highest Christian attainments here,— it will be through revivals.

How do revivals come?

They are given by God, not created by men. They are produced by the spontaneous movements of that sovereign Spirit, Who, like the wind, "bloweth as He listeth." They are not produced by human efforts. But God loves to work through means; and He has made the visitations of His grace dependent, for the most part, upon certain action on the part of His people. To say that a revival may at any time be secured by the use of the right means, is not to limit the sovereignty of God; for it is He Who gives the disposition to use the means. To say that a revival may *not* be secured at any time by the use of the right means, is to cast discredit upon the promises. If, then, a greatly needed revival fails to come, some of us are in fault. Who is it? Is it *you?*

Do you want one?

Undoubtedly your answer is, Yes. You would like to see a great revival in progress; you often pray, "O Lord, revive Thy work;" "Pour out Thy Spirit upon us." But are you in earnest? Do you mean what you say? How much do you want a revival? There is, certainly, need enough of a revival. Worldliness and sloth have half paralyzed the Churches; the love of many has grown cold, they have forgotten their first love; infidelity and idolatry and wickedness are rapidly increasing around us; vast multitudes are living near us without God, and passing in endless procession from us to His bar to be condemned and punished for ever. You have personal reasons for desiring a revival; your own soul needs to be refreshed with a new anointing from on high; you have very dear friends, and not a few of them, of whom you know that there is no reasonable hope that they will ever be converted and saved from the wrath to come, unless in a revival. Are your desires for a revival proportioned to the urgency of the need? Is there an earnestness in your prayers, springing out of a conviction that some of your best friends are on the brink of hell? Does the condition of the community rest with an insupportable weight upon your heart? Some years ago, one said, "I feel, that, if we do not have a revival soon, I shall die!" Is that your feeling? Are you crying mightily unto God, if so be that we perish not, or are you asleep in the sides of the ship? How much are you willing to do and sacrifice in order to secure a revival?

Will you help to secure a revival?

In reply, you ask, "What must I do?"

1. *You must prepare your own heart.*

If you had grieved your own father, and driven him away from your dwelling, by disregarding his wishes and contemning his person, and introducing into your home companions and occupations and scenes that he abhorred, and if you wished to have him again visit you, you would humble yourself, you would ask forgiveness, you would show contrition; and you would put away all that he abhorred, you would assure him that he might return without fear of finding in your house the things which were offensive to him. If you wish the Spirit to come, you must humble yourself before God, you must confess your sins with sincere sorrow and abhorrence for them, you must seek forgiveness anew through the blood of Jesus; and you must not only humble yourself, you must put away evil. When Jacob went up to Bethel to meet God, his command to his family was, "Put away the strange gods, and be clean, and change your garments." Before God would come down to Israel on Sinai, they had to sanctify themselves, and wash their clothes. If you wish for a visit from the Spirit, you must put away evil. If you are angry with any one, you must become reconciled to him. If you have wronged any one, you must go to him and "confess your faults" frankly, humbly, and whether there has been wrong on his part or no, and whether there is penitence in him or no. And not only so, but you must, so far as possible, make *restitution,* prompt, cheerful, and complete. You cannot be forgiven the wrong, while you still possess that for which you did the wrong.

" May one be pardoned, and retain th' offence? "

You cannot clear yourself till you have restored, and, like Zaccheus, "fourfold." If you have neglected any duty, you must take it up. If you are indulging in any forbidden pleasure, or in any sin, open or secret, you must drop it. If you have set your affections upon social position, property, reputation, or any worldly eminence, and have in thought and conduct bowed down to the creature, you must tear from the throne of your heart the dearest and every idol. If you do not, the Spirit will not visit you, and perhaps he will not visit your Church. By secretly taking some of the forbidden spoil, Achan took the victory from the banners of Israel, and "troubled" the people of God. Who is it, that, by his secret lust after the things of this world, is preventing the Lord from going forth with His people, and hindering the triumphs of His grace? Is it *you?*

2. *You must apply yourself to seeking and expecting the Spirit.*

Suppose, that, when Jesus was on earth, He had come one day to a village, and had found, that, although His coming had been expected, yet the villagers, instead of being all gathered "waiting for Him," were all scattered, "one to his farm and another to his merchandise," one to his shop and another to his net, some to the amphitheatre to see the sports and others to a feast to mingle in the revels. Do you think that He could have tarried long, or done there "many mighty works"? Do you imagine that there would ever have been any Pentecost, if the disciples, instead of all "continuing with one accord in one place," had been scattered, some to their business and some to their amusements, these to the temple and those to the palace? Revivals usually commence, and exert their greatest power, in public religious assemblies. If you want a revival, you must, for the time, leave concerts and lectures, operas and plays, dinners and parties, whether they are right or wrong, innocent or injurious; you must, for the time, give up as much as you consistently can of your business and daily occupation, and resort to the assemblies of the people of God,—to where the multitudes are waiting and praying for the promise of the Father. Suppose that *all* the members of one Church should begin with one accord to meet together in one place in prayer and supplication; have you the least doubt what the speedy result would be? And can you for slight cause absent yourself? And suppose that every one should be ready with some exhortation or prayer; do you not know that the effect of the very first meeting would be electric? And yet you can sit silent! But you "have not the talent." Possibly you are hiding it. But grant it; you can, at least, pray. There never yet was one whose heart the Lord had touched, who was unable to speak *to Him*. Forget that there are others around you; see "no man save Jesus only." Oh, these silent Christians! Do you know the distinguishing characteristic of the guest who had not on the wedding-garment? "HE WAS SPEECHLESS."

3. *You must sustain the right kind of preaching.*

Truth, and truth presented in public address, is a mighty and chosen instrument of God for reaching the consciences and hearts of men.

But it is not every kind of preaching which tends to produce a revival. It is not by elaborate periods of eloquence, by graphic descriptions, by flights of poetry, by theological discussions, by political tirades, by moral lectures, by literary essays, or by pious remarks, that sinners are ever going to be awakened and converted. This can only be accomplished by the tender and affectionate, but simple, plain, direct, forcible presentations of the truths of the Gospel, the holiness of God, the wickedness of the natural heart, the judgment, and wrath to come, pardon and salvation through the crucified Saviour, the guilt of resisting the Holy Ghost, the unsearchable riches of Christ; and by kind and meek, but yet plain and severe rebukes of every form of sin, and earnest pleadings for practical holiness. Is this the kind of preaching that you want to hear? Will you sustain God's ministers in it? Will you even *demand* that the preaching of the word of life to dying men shall be of that stamp? Or are you restive and impatient under it, disposed to depreciate and speak against it, angry and defiant when your own conscience is disturbed? How much do you want a revival? Perhaps you would rather that your minister should preach poetical and ingenious and smooth and pleasant things, and that your friends should slumber on undisturbed till they awake in hell.

4. *You must* PRAY *for a revival.*

How rich the promises! "If ye, being evil, know how to give good gifts unto your children, how much more shall your heavenly Father give the Holy Spirit to them that ask Him!"

"Ask, and ye shall receive; seek, and ye shall find; knock, and it shall be opened unto you."

You *do*, often, pray for the out-pouring of the Spirit. Yes, but *how?*

It is not the occasional repetition of the hackneyed phrases of the prayer-meeting, which is to bring a revival. In every meeting for prayer, every time that you kneel at the family altar, every time that you go to your closet, as often as your heart ascends to the throne of grace, you must pray for a revival; and that, not with cold and formal words, but with the earnestness of a heart that is oppressed and wearied and aching with the burden of perishing souls, with a profound sense of the dependence of man upon the grace of God, with an unwavering faith in the promises, with the pleadings of a bleeding heart, and a "soul breaking for the longing that it hath at all times," "with strong crying and tears unto Him that is able to save," "with groanings that cannot be uttered." *Do you know* HOW *to pray?* How would you plead with the Governor for a father or a son condemned to die? And what will you say to God for dear ones whom He may this very night, not deliver unto death, but "cast soul and body into hell"?

5. *You must* WORK *for a revival.*

It is true that God only can convert. He sends the quickening light and showers; but man must sow the seed. Is it not wonderful presumption which enables us, after having done not one thing to lead any soul to Christ, to go to God, and coolly pray, in measured tones, "Revive Thy work"? What tender and almighty pity that holds back the thunderbolts from those who burn such strange incense before Him!

You have an unconverted brother: go and tell him that you have "found the Christ," and bid him "come and see." You have young men in your employ: "run, speak to that young man." You have a class in the Sabbath School: point the children plainly, tenderly, to the great Shepherd. You have a beloved friend who is still unreconciled to God: go and talk with him, tremblingly, it may be, but faithfully, affectionately, tearfully. Or, if you have reason to fear that your words may do more harm than good, seek to bring other influences to bear upon him, or, at least, go and tell Jesus. But be not too timid. It may be that he is waiting and wishing for some one to take him by the hand, and lead him to Christ, and wondering that "no man cares for his soul." Speak to Christians as well as to the unconverted; it may be that you will encourage, quicken, reclaim, comfort, or strengthen something that is "ready to die." If you have received any thing, if you hope for any thing from the Lord, improve every suitable opportunity, *watch* for opportunities, *make* opportunities, to speak for Jesus! Tell " every morning of His loving kindness, every night of His faithfulness." Oh, the words that we speak for Jesus cannot die; though they may seem to accomplish nothing here, they will come back to us hereafter in everlasting strains of music. Let your every going forth be that of a sower of the word. "In the morning sow thy seed, and in the evening withhold not thine hand; for thou knowest not whether shall prosper either this or that, or whether they both shall be alike good." Cast it on the "troubled sea," as well as on the good ground, and in likeliest spots: it may be that you will find it after many days. It is not possible that God should withhold all increase from the planting of love and the watering of tears. "He that goeth forth, *and weepeth*, bearing precious seed, shall doubtless return again with joy, bringing his sheaves with him." But if, with all your labors and prayers, you shall fail to secure a revival, or even the salvation of a single soul, you will, at least, win the approbation, yes, the *gratitude*, of Christ; and when you come to stand before Him, and bathe His feet with tears of disappointment in having been able to accomplish little for Him, you will hear from His lips some such words of loving praise and everlasting welcome, and recommendation to the deepest and tenderest sympathies of His followers, as He pronounced over her who anointed His body for its burial,— "She hath done what she could."

Addresses to Church Members

BY THE

CONGREGATIONAL PASTORS OF BOSTON,

RECOMMENDED BY THE

Boston Congregational Council.

The following are now published, and ready for delivery: —

No. 1. THE RESULT OF COUNCIL. Complete.

No. 2. THE CHRISTIAN'S RECONSECRATION. By Rev. E. K. ALDEN, Pastor of Phillips Church.

No. 3. THE WORLDLINESS OF NOMINAL CHRISTIANS. By Rev. Dr. WEBB, Pastor of Shawmut Church.

No. 4. THE DUTY OF CHRISTIANS TO UNITE WITH SOME CHURCH, AND THE DUTY OF CHURCH-MEMBERS TO UNITE WITH THE CHURCH WHERE THEY STATEDLY WORSHIP. By Rev. S. P. FAY, Pastor of Salem Church.

THE DUTY OF DAILY SECRET PRAYER and DAILY STUDY OF THE BIBLE. By Rev. J. M. MANNING.

REVIVALS OF RELIGION. By Rev. J. E. TODD.

The remaining Addresses will follow at intervals of about one week; viz: —

THE SPREAD OF THE GOSPEL IN THE CITY AMONG THE POOR, AND THOSE WHO HABITUALLY NEGLECT THE SERVICES OF THE SABBATH. By Rev. Dr. DEXTER.

THE CHRISTIAN'S DUTY TO WORK FOR THE SAVING OF SOULS. By Rev. Mr. BINGHAM.

THE DUTY OF A MORE STRICT OBSERVANCE OF THE SABBATH. By Rev. Dr. BLAGDEN.

THE POWER AND OFFICE OF THE HOLY SPIRIT. By Rev. Dr. ADAMS.

THE POWER OF PRAYER. By Rev. Dr. KIRK.

THE DIVINE SOVEREIGNTY IN ITS RELATION TO HUMAN SALVATION. By Rev. Mr. BAKER.

No. 7. *Published by direction of the Congregational Churches of Boston.*

DIVINE SOVEREIGNTY

IN

HUMAN SALVATION.

BY

REV. A. R. BAKER.

BOSTON:
NICHOLS AND NOYES.
1866.

DIVINE SOVEREIGNTY

IN

HUMAN SALVATION.

BY

Rev. A. R. BAKER.

BOSTON:
NICHOLS AND NOYES.
1866.

Entered according to Act of Congress, in the year 1866, by

NICHOLS AND NOYES,

In the Clerk's Office of the District Court of the District of Massachusetts.

CAMBRIDGE:
STEREOTYPED AND PRINTED BY JOHN WILSON AND SONS.

DIVINE SOVEREIGNTY
IN
HUMAN SALVATION.

What is the sovereignty of God?

SOVEREIGNTY enters into the very idea of government, which, within its own sphere, has one, and can have but one, highest power, one supreme authority. This may exist in an individual, or in a plurality of persons. In every well-regulated household, it is in the head of the family, whose laws are exempt from foreign control, subordinate only to those of the State and of God, and demand prompt and implicit obedience. In schools and seminaries of learning, it resides in the Principal, who is responsible to the supervisors of education, and to those for whom they act. In the Commonwealth, it is vested in the Governor, who approves and authenticates, or defeats, the bills of the Legislature; who signs and executes, commutes or remits, the sentences of the Judges; who affixes the seal of the State to the commission of its subordinate officers, and gives them authority. In the Republic, it is exercised by the President, who, in addition to all such acts which he performs for the nation, commands her army and navy, pardons or punishes transgressors of her laws. In the world, it is in God, Who "works all things after the counsel of His will," and Who "does according to His pleasure in the army of heaven and among the inhabitants of the earth."

This is His Own definition, from which we learn that God's sovereignty is not caprice, or action without good reason; nor arbitrariness, or action for the mere display of authority: but it is intelligent action, exhibiting the will of the highest power. Divine sovereignty is God's government of the world according to His will, so as to fulfil His purpose in all creatures and events; it implies "His perfect right to govern and dispose of them in conformity with His Own good pleasure." It also implies God's right to command, and our duty to obey. In respect to the system of redemption, to the salvation of men, His language is more precise and specific: " I will have mercy on whom I will have mercy; and I will have compassion on whom I will have compassion. So, then, it is not of him that walketh, nor of him that runneth, but of God that sheweth mercy." Here sovereignty is exercised in pardoning the guilty, saving the lost.

But what are the characteristics of Divine sovereignty?

In a family, a school, a state, and in every government, we learn the character and plan of the sovereign from his own declarations and acts. Thus we call Tarquin, the Proud; Julian, the Cruel; Job, the Patient Man; Abraham, the Faithful; Solomon, the Wise.

So the sovereignty of God bears the impress of His Own character,—holy, wise, and powerful. It is intelligent, for " His understanding is infinite;" powerful, for He is " almighty;" universal, for He " filleth all in all;" uniform, for He is " the same yesterday, to-day, and for ever;" wise, for He abounds " in all wisdom and prudence;" faithful, for He always fulfils His promises and threatenings; righteous, for "He sitteth upon the throne of His holiness;" benevolent, for "He is good," supremely good, and "His tender mercies are over all His works;" compassionate, for "His mercy endureth for ever;" glorious, for He is "the King of glory;" praiseworthy: "Let every thing that hath breath praise the Lord," and all may shout, with the heavenly hosts, "Alleluia; salvation, and glory, and honor, and power, be unto the Lord our God." Such is the adorable sovereignty of God.

But does He reign supreme in the kingdom of grace?

It is eminently desirable that God should rule in this kingdom, with a comprehensiveness embracing the whole plan, with a minuteness extending to every son and daughter of Adam, to every display of His mercy towards each of them. What would you not give to have these qualities always distinguish the sovereignty that rules your family, sanctifying your social relations, multiplying and sweetening the joys of home; converting your habitation into a Bethel, into "the gate of heaven"? What a blessing, if you could have such sovereignty preside over the schools which you attend or sustain! How it would aid the acquisition and communication of knowledge; lighten or remove the burden of discipline; and subordinate education, in the largest, best sense of that word, to the wisest and most benevolent of purposes! If you knew that such sovereignty would always preside over the nation, how that assurance would relieve the fears of your loyal heart, and confirm your faith in the ultimate attainment of the highest consistent welfare of each citizen and of the whole nation! Any people, blessed with the right of elective franchise, would act wisely in choosing a person possessed, as far as possible, of such qualities to rule over them. None but bad men and criminals fear the legitimate exercise of such authority.

You cannot but esteem it a blessing that a sovereign God has created and rules the material universe; — the clouds which are His chariot; the stormy wind which He directs; the ocean that rolls in the hollow of His hand; the sun, moon, and stars that shine to His praise; "Arcturus, Orion, Pleiades, and the chambers of the south" which He made; all planets and systems revolving harmoniously at His command : yea, that He governs all the objects of nature, from the falling of a hair to the destruction of a world ; and all the events of providence, however trivial or momentous in our esteem. All things are open to His inspection ; all, subject to His control. "Thou, even Thou, art Lord alone ; Thou hast made heaven, the heaven of heavens, with all their hosts ; the earth, and all things that are therein ; and thou preservest them all ; and the host of heaven worshippeth Thee."

It is much more desirable that this adorable Sovereign should reign in the kingdom of grace, to which both nature and providence are subservient. These are but the scaffolding of God's temple, to be removed when its head-stone shall have been laid with shouting, " Grace, grace unto it ; " when Jesus, Who " holds the stars in His right hand," and " walks among the golden candlesticks," shall have put down all rule, and all authority and power ; and when " every creature in heaven and on earth and under the earth, and such as are in the sea, and all that are in them, shall be heard, saying, 'Blessing, and honor, and glory, and power, be unto Him that sitteth upon the throne, and unto the Lamb for ever and ever.'" Then Christ will appear as He is in truth, "all in all;" and salvation by His grace, the end for which the sovereign Ruler made and governs all things, the theme most worthy the aspirations and endeavors of mankind and the praise of "the just made perfect."

Every child of God looks on the land and sea, on the starry heavens, and the various objects of nature, and sings, "My Father made them all." He sees God's hand in every event of providence; and, though "clouds and darkness are" sometimes "round about Him," he rests on the assurance, "righteousness and judgment are the habitation of His throne." In his devotions, he acknowledges and celebrates sovereign grace, which transformed him from a "vessel of wrath" into one of mercy, from an enemy to a friend, from an alien to a child and heir. He prays with David, " Uphold me with Thy free Spirit; then will I teach transgressors Thy ways, and sinners shall be converted unto Thee." With the beloved disciple, he says, I was " born, not of blood, nor of the will of the flesh, nor of the will of man, but of God." He cries, with Paul, " It is not of him

1*

that willeth, nor of him that runneth, but of God that showeth mercy."—"Hath not the potter power over the clay, of the same lump to make one vessel unto honor and another unto dishonor?"—"We are His workmanship, created in Christ Jesus unto good works." We are enabled " to will and also to do of His good pleasure." With intensity of emotion, he repeats the words of his Divine Master, "I can of Mine Own Self do nothing;" but adds, with the apostle, "I can do all things through Christ Which strengtheneth me."

Christ, then, is "Head over all things to the Church." He is "the true Vine," imparting to each branch life and productiveness; the Alpha and Omega of every man's salvation. God is a Sovereign in the kingdom of grace, as well as in nature and providence.

But how is His sovereignty displayed in our salvation?

1. *By the gracious plan* which His wisdom devised, His love adopted, His faithfulness and grace carry steadily onward, and are pledged to consummate. We, His intelligent creatures, act

by design. If we are faithful parents, we educate our children, and settle them according to the purposes of our wisdom and love. Are we to construct for ourselves a habitation? We make known our wants to an architect, who draws a plan which we adopt and execute. "Every house is builded by some man; but He that built all things is God." But, if we build houses and ships by plans and according to purposes previously adopted, shall we not concede to God the right to form and govern the world and the Church according to the counsel of His mind? The patriarch of Uz says of God, "What His soul desireth, even that He doeth." God Himself adds, "My counsel shall stand; and I will do all My pleasure."

But, respecting the system of grace and mediation, the Bible is full and explicit: "Moreover, whom He did predestinate, them He also called; and whom He called, them He also justified; and whom He justified, them He also glorified." Every step in the process of sa'vation develops His plan, and teaches the good pleasure of His will. So reasoned the apostle, who contemplated this theme, as we should do, with wonder and admiration: "Blessed be the God and Father of our Lord Jesus Christ, Who hath blessed us with all spiritual blessings in heavenly places in Christ, according as He hath chosen us in Him, before the foundation of the world, that we should be holy and without blame before Him in love; having predestinated us unto the adoption of children by Jesus Christ to Himself, according to the good pleasure of His will, to the praise of the glory of His grace." If any thing can move the soul to its lowest depths, it is the thought that God so loved it from eternity, and out of His mere good pleasure, as to cherish toward it designs of mercy, and to adopt a plan whereby it may be saved, may sing and shine before Him for ever and ever. In the formation of that plan, God had no counsellor, but acted in the exercise of His adorable sovereignty.

2. But this is also displayed *by the covenants* which He formed and revealed in fulfilment of His plan. These are reducible to two,—the covenant of works, and the covenant of grace. In the first of these, He formed angels, created mankind, and proffered eternal life on condition of perfect obedience. What the law says to one,

it says to all: He that obeyeth shall live (Gal. iii. 12); but "the soul that sinneth, it shall die" (Ezek. xviii. 20). Lucifer and others of the heavenly host fell from the privileges of this Divine constitution. So also did our first parents. By their "disobedience," "many were made sinners;" that is, all their posterity were corrupted, constituted sinners, and brought under the wrath and curse of a broken law, so ruined that no works of future obedience could save them. Here, whatever link you strike, the tenth or ten thousandth breaks the chain alike. "By the deeds of the law shall no flesh be justified." "All have sinned, and come short of the glory of God."

Sin ruined this provision for human salvation. But God's love did what it always intended to do: it promulgated a system of mediation, a covenant of grace in which eternal life is freely offered us, and even urged upon our acceptance, on condition of faith. "By grace are ye saved through faith, and that not of yourselves: it is the gift of God."

Of these two covenants, the first admitted of no modification, but was complete from the moment of its proclamation. The second was gradually developed; it rose and increased like the king of day. Adam and the antediluvians saw only the morning star of redemption; Abraham and other patriarchs, the early dawn; Moses and the prophets, the brightening light; while the disciples of Christ behold "the Sun of righteousness," rising and shining in the greatness of His strength.

Hear how God speaks of justification by each of these covenants: "Moses describeth the righteousness which is of the law, that the man which doeth these things shall live by them. But the righteousness which is of faith speaketh on this wise. . . . If thou shalt confess with thy mouth the Lord Jesus, and shalt believe in thine heart that God hath raised Him from the dead, thou shalt be saved." Of each covenant salvation is the end. Both were adopted out of His mere good pleasure, and express His holy sovereignty. "God, willing to show His wrath and to make His power known, endured with much long-suffering the vessels of wrath fitted to destruction, that he might make known the riches of His glory, on the vessels of mercy." Mark the words: "endured with much long-suffering" the guilt and misery of some of His accountable creatures that He might more clearly reveal His glorious sovereignty in the salvation of others; even as the sun, in his march through the heavens, appears brighter in contrast with the dark spots on his disk. Like prisons and dungeons in civil government, hell is a dark spot in the universe; but it is necessary for persistent covenant-breakers; sovereignty subordinates it to the highest general good: and therefore all may sing, "Alleluia; for the Lord God omnipotent reigneth."

3. The adorable sovereignty of God appointed *Christ the Mediator* of the covenant of grace. Sin cut us off from access to God, from His favor that is life, and His loving kindness that is better than life. God would deliver us; but how could He, without the subversion of supreme authority, the compromise of right, the evasion of the threatened penalty? We needed some one to satisfy for our offences, to atone for our sins, and to procure for us free forgiveness. All had sinned; not one of the human race could make

satisfaction for the rest. Angels could not; for they must keep the law constantly and perfectly, to secure their own salvation. Who could or would undertake the mighty work?

When God inquired, "Whom shall I send, and who will go for Us?" His eternal Son replied, "Here am I: send Me." God, in the exercise of His holy sovereignty, "laid help upon One that is mighty," "Jesus Christ the righteous." He chose and appointed Him our Mediator, a Day's-man, an Umpire between Himself and us,—human, and therefore able to comprehend our guilt and misery imputed to Him; Divine, and therefore capable of understanding perfectly the claims to be met and satisfied; Immanuel, the God-man who laid one hand on the throne and the other on the footstool, and became the way perfect and entire, whereby Divine mercy could be consistently conveyed to us, and our prayers and praises ascend to Him. "Such an High Priest became us, Who is holy, harmless, undefiled, separate from sinners, and made higher than the heavens; Who needeth not daily, as other high priests, to offer up sacrifice, first for His Own sins, and then for the people's: for this He did once, when He offered up Himself." "Him God set forth to be a propitiation, to declare His righteousness for the remission" of our sins. He died our death, and exhausted our curse, that we might be made the righteousness of God in Him, and that God might be just, and yet justify us miserable offenders. We adore the sovereignty which selected Him for our Mediator, the only Personage that could make an atonement for our sins; and when we think of Him laying aside the glory He had with the Father before the world was, veiling His divinity with humanity, suffering, praying, groaning, bleeding, dying for our sins, rising for our justification, ascending to heaven, and preparing mansions for our everlasting abode, we exclaim, with the chief of the apostles, "Oh, the depth of the riches, both of the wisdom and knowledge of God!"

4. *Sovereignty selected fallen men, rather than apostate angels, to be the objects of Divine mercy.*

Angels existed before the creation of mankind; for, when God laid the corner-stone and foundation of this world, they celebrated the event. "The morning stars sang together, and all the sons of God shouted for joy." In the scale of being, they were originally exalted far above us, and probably possessed minds endowed with faculties more enlarged, knowledge and wisdom more profound; and they were capable of service more pure and exalted. Why, then, did God pass by the angels who fell, and "whom He hath reserved in everlasting chains under darkness unto the judgment of the great day," and provide redemption for mankind? Why took Christ on Him the nature, not of angels, but of the seed of Abraham? Reason and speculate as we may on these questions, they resolve themselves at last into this: "Even so, Father; for so it seemed good in Thy sight."

5. The amiable sovereignty of God fixed *the simplest conditions to our pardon and eternal life.*

It is the prerogative of the highest power to specify the terms on which its clemency may be enjoyed. This belongs to parents in the family, to the Governor in the state, to the President in the nation. And that power displays its magnanimity and glory by making the terms as simple and easy of compliance as may be consistent with the general good and the personal welfare of its subject. If a parent forgives his disobedient child without a confession of his fault and a pledge of reformation, he weakens family government, and encourages waywardness. If a chief magistrate pardons criminals while a spirit of insubordination still reigns in their hearts, it is presumption for him to expect social order and general tranquillity in the nation. So in the moral government of God, and under the reign of grace, we who have sinned cannot enjoy the smile of Divine favor, till we "put away sin by righteousness, and iniquity by turning unto the Lord;" till our rebellion against God is succeeded by loyalty to Him; till our impenitence yields to godly sorrow, our unbelief to a childlike trust, our carnality to spirituality, our heart of stone to one of flesh. Therefore God's sovereignty, which commands us to make a new heart and a new spirit, to repent, believe, and obey the Gospel, speaks with the wisest reference to our good, to the welfare of Christ's kingdom and to the glory of the Lord. It specifies the simplest conditions on which grace can be received and enjoyed. As the drunkard must reform before he can inherit the blessings which reward temperance, so every sinner must become holy, his heart must beat in unison with God's; he must love what God loves, and hate what He hates; and he himself must be refashioned in the moral image which he lost by the fall, or he cannot enter the kingdom of heaven. Through this gate every man must pass or perish.

6. Out of His mere good pleasure, God sent *His Spirit to dispose and enable us to comply with these conditions of life everlasting.*

Sin has so debased and enfeebled us that we cannot do the good we would. "Ye cannot serve the Lord; for He is a holy God." Of yourself alone, you cannot make you a new heart, repent, believe, or obey the Gospel. The Saviour says, "No man can come to Me, except the Father Which hath sent Me draw him." He draws you by His Spirit, by the prayers of His people, by the institutions of religion, and the means of grace.

If you imagine you are both able and willing

to perform these duties, make the attempt; and the experiment will be likely to convince you that you must have such help as the Holy Spirit alone can render. The Bible compares this Divine Helper to the wind or atmosphere which circles and pervades every material object, but which you must inhale in order to sustain your animal life.

Yet God was under no obligation to send you His Spirit; or, having sent it, to continue His gracious strivings a moment, especially after your grieving and resisting Him. The gift and operation of the Spirit are expressions of Divine sovereignty: so, too, are all His whispers in the recesses of your mind, all His calls to repentance, all His impulses to faith, all His motives to obedience, all His earnest pleadings by the voice of providence, and the living ministry, all the intercessions which He inspired in your behalf. Each of these is a witness of His good pleasure, a fresh proclamation of His desire for your salvation, a new endeavor to lead you to Christ, to give you the new heart which you are commanded to make, the repentance and faith which you are required to put forth, and the salvation which you should work out; for it is God that worketh in you and with you, and disposes and enables you to work out obedience.

7. In the exercise of His holy sovereignty, God makes *distinctions in the display of His grace.*

He chose Noah, before other antediluvians, to preserve His Church from the flood; formed His covenant with Abraham, rather than with any of his contemporaries; called the Jews, in preference to other nations, to be His peculiar people; chose David, out of the sons of Jesse, to rule His kingdom; Mary to be the mother of the infant Saviour; Paul, before other persecutors, to become the chief of the apostles; Christians at Antioch, before other disciples, to commence Foreign Missions.

In the economy of His grace, does He not now do more for our nation than for the tribes of Central Africa; more for one church, family, and individual than for another? Does any one doubt whether he bestowed grace on John, the beloved disciple, not received by Judas Iscariot? Now, as of old, what diversity in the endowments of God's people! By the same

Spirit, "to one is given the word of wisdom; to another, the word of knowledge; to another, the working of miracles; to another, prophecy; to another, discerning of spirits; to another, divers kinds of tongues: to every man severally as He will." He imparts to one convert a quicker perception of sin; to a second, more adorable views of Christ; to a third, clearer and more comprehensive conceptions of the plan and covenants of God; to a fourth, overflowing love; to a fifth, stronger faith; to a sixth, a larger measure of humility; to a seventh, more steadfastness or zeal. There are " diversities of operation, but the same Spirit working all in all," and calling each to improve his peculiar gifts, and to perform the special service for which they qualify him. All such distinctions display His sovereign grace, and prepare each of its subjects for the part he is to sing in the new song of heaven.

Who will not rejoice in the display of Divine sovereignty in human salvation?

Has not God a right to do what He will with His Own? Had He not a perfect right to create the world according to His eternal purpose? — to form both angels and men, and to endow the mind of each according to the good pleasure of His will? — to place them all under the covenant of works? — and, when they fell by sinning against Him, to reveal to mankind a system of grace? — to elect His Own Son as our Mediator? — to allow Him to become incarnate, to suffer and die, for our redemption? God Himself asks, "Is thine eye evil because I am good?" Who doubts His right to pass by the angels that fell, and to show mercy to men? to offer salvation to you and to me on the simplest possible conditions? to send His Spirit to help us comply with the terms of pardon and eternal life? to make or to allow all the distinctions which we witness in the display of grace? Why, then, should any object to His sovereignty in our salvation?

Is its action *mysterious?* Of course, the finite cannot embrace the Infinite. Yet we believe and act constantly on what we very imperfectly comprehend. We know not how our body and soul are united in one person; but we believe the fact of that union, and daily act upon it. In our childhood, we could not always comprehend the principles on which our parents issued their commands; but our confidence, working by love, prompted obedience. "Shall we not much rather be in subjection unto the Father of spirits, and live?"

How can God's sovereignty make Him appear a *partial* Being? He has clearly revealed His will; He sincerely invites all to accept proffered mercy; He gave His Son to redeem and save the lost, sent His Spirit and commissioned His Church to call mankind, and is faithful in the execution of His promises and threatenings. He nowhere approves of sin, but suffers it for a season to exist, even as wise earthly rulers sometimes allow the transgression of their laws for a short period, either in the hope of overcoming evil with good, or to render more manifest the necessity and justice of punishment. He treats all men better than they deserve, and has good and sufficient reasons for all the distinction which He makes in the economy of His grace. If any unreconciled heart object, inspiration answers, "Nay, O man, who art thou that repliest against God? Shall the thing formed say to Him that formed it, Why hast Thou made me thus?" Underlying this objection is the old man, which is corrupt, and in arms against his supreme Ruler. "Let the potsherd strive with the potsherds of the earth; but woe to him that striveth with his Maker!" He must surrender, or perish.

Does the sovereignty of God in salvation interfere with *the freedom of man?* No; as well ask, whether the laws of the solar system, and the revolution of the planets, interfere with the activity of the inhabitants of the earth; whether the currents of the ocean hinder the action of the fish that swim therein; whether the wind prevents the flight of birds through the air; whether the plan of a campaign destroys the responsibility of the officers and men who execute it; whether the authority of a wise and loving father suspends the personal accountability of his own offspring. When parents live and act in their children, earthly rulers in their subjects, think it not strange that "God works in us to will and to do of His good pleasure." You are to work out what He works in you. Let His promise encourage, sustain, and crown with success, your endeavors to obtain eternal life.

What are the special duties to which the sovereignty of God in salvation now calls you?

A faithful use of all the means of grace. These are the tools of this Divine art, the appointed instruments of salvation, by which a sovereign God works in you the salvation which He requires you to work out " with fear and trembling." If you are a believer, and would mature your faith and piety; or if you are an unbeliever, " without God and without hope in the world," and would be saved by Christ and His gospel, — sanctify the Sabbath, remembering the day to keep it holy. Attend regularly and faithfully public worship, " in season and out of season ; " for " Thy way, O God, is in the sanctuary," — His way of instruction in Divine knowledge, of consolation, and of salvation. " Search the Scriptures; for in them ye think ye have eternal life." Like the Bereans, try the sermons you hear by this Divine standard, appealing " to the law and to the testimony ; if they speak not according to this word, it is because there is no truth in them." Pray, like the poor publican, " God be merciful to me a sinner ; " for every one who asks in such a spirit is heard and blessed.

But God's adorable sovereignty in salvation calls you to comply *with the conditions of mercy.* Your inviting Saviour cries in your ear, "Come unto Me;" "take My yoke upon you:" that is, "Submit yourself as a loyal subject unto My government; yield your will in sweet submission to Mine; confess and forsake your sins; return unto Me, and I will return unto you. Repent, believe, and obey the gospel: for 'behold, now is the accepted time; behold, now is the day of salvation.'" If you verbally or practically reply, "No, not *now*," you really, and so long as you continue of the same mind, rebel against His supreme authority; you return His ocean love with hatred; you hinder prayer in your behalf; you resist and grieve His waiting, striving Spirit. Every moment you do this, you hazard your soul; that lost, what can you account gain? All is lost, — irrecoverably and for ever lost!

But you need not, you must not, longer incur that awful risk; you must not allow the favored moment, "big with mercy," to pass unimproved, and to force from you the lamentation, "The harvest is passed, the summer is ended, and I am not saved." God forbids it; "the Spirit and the

Bride" forbid it; your own reason and conscience forbid it.

Come, like the prodigal, to your offended Sovereign, and say, "Father, I have sinned against heaven and before Thee, and am no more worthy to be called Thy son: make me as one of Thy hired servants." Then He will meet and embrace you, will make you His child and heir; heaven will rejoice; and you yourself will join in the song, "Worthy is the Lamb!"

Addresses to Church Members

BY THE

CONGREGATIONAL PASTORS OF BOSTON,

RECOMMENDED BY THE

Boston Congregational Council.

The following are now published, and ready for delivery:—

No. 1. THE RESULT OF COUNCIL. Complete.

No. 2. THE CHRISTIAN'S RECONSECRATION. By Rev. E. K. ALDEN, Pastor of Phillips Church.

No. 3. THE WORLDLINESS OF NOMINAL CHRISTIANS. By Rev. Dr. WEBB, Pastor of Shawmut Church.

No. 4. THE DUTY OF CHRISTIANS TO UNITE WITH SOME CHURCH, AND THE DUTY OF CHURCH-MEMBERS TO UNITE WITH THE CHURCH WHERE THEY STATEDLY WORSHIP. By Rev. S. P. FAY, Pastor of Salem Church.

No. 5. THE DUTY OF DAILY SECRET PRAYER and DAILY STUDY OF THE BIBLE. By Rev. J. M. MANNING.

No. 6. REVIVALS OF RELIGION. By Rev. J. E. TODD.

No. 7. THE DIVINE SOVEREIGNTY IN ITS RELATION TO HUMAN SALVATION. By Rev. Mr. BAKER.

The remaining Addresses will follow at intervals of about one week; viz:—

THE SPREAD OF THE GOSPEL IN THE CITY AMONG THE POOR, AND THOSE WHO HABITUALLY NEGLECT THE SERVICES OF THE SABBATH. By Rev. Dr. DEXTER.

THE CHRISTIAN'S DUTY TO WORK FOR THE SAVING OF SOULS. By Rev. Mr. BINGHAM.

THE DUTY OF A MORE STRICT OBSERVANCE OF THE SABBATH. By Rev. Dr. BLAGDEN.

THE POWER AND OFFICE OF THE HOLY SPIRIT. By Rev. Dr. ADAMS.

THE POWER OF PRAYER. By Rev. Dr. KIRK.

THE DUTY

OF

A MORE STRICT OBSERVANCE
OF THE SABBATH.

BY

Rev G. W. BLAGDEN, D.D.

BOSTON:

THE DUTY

OF

A MORE STRICT OBSERVANCE
OF THE SABBATH.

BY

Rev. G. W. BLAGDEN, D.D.

BOSTON:
NICHOLS AND NOYES.
1866.

Entered according to Act of Congress, in the year 1866, by

NICHOLS AND NOYES,

In the Clerk's Office of the District Court of the District of Massachusetts.

CAMBRIDGE:
STEREOTYPED AND PRINTED BY JOHN WILSON AND SONS.

THE DUTY OF A MORE STRICT OBSERVANCE OF THE SABBATH.

Is the keeping of the Sabbath, now, commanded by Divine authority; or, is it only a duty required by a wise expediency, but not Divinely, and absolutely, commanded under the Gospel of Christ?

In reply to this inquiry, I shall try to show that the remembrance of the Sabbath day, "to keep it holy," is now required of all believers in Jesus, by the law of God as it is magnified and made honorable in the Gospel; and that the manner in which this is done leads us to right conclusions respecting the ways in which we should fulfil "the duty of a more strict observance of the day."

I. The Lord Jesus declared, on one occasion, that the "Son of Man is Lord of the Sabbath day." What does such a declaration imply?

It implies that Jesus, as the Son of man, possessed and exercised authority to regulate the keeping of the Sabbath. He spoke the words in asserting His authority to do this, for He was then correcting the false views the Pharisees entertained of its observance. They supposed it unlawful for His disciples, in passing through the corn-fields on the Sabbath, — when engaged with Him, their Lord and Master, in works of love and mercy to men, — to pluck the ears of corn and satisfy their hunger. But He assured them, from facts in their own history, that the spirit of the law of the Sabbath permitted such necessary acts. He alluded to the act of David and those who were with him, in entering, when they were an hungered, the house of God, and eating the shewbread, which it was lawful, commonly, for only the priests to eat; and He cited the conduct of the priests as being harmless, when they, on the Sabbath day, did certain acts which might seem to profane it, — thus showing His hearers, as He is recorded in the Gospel of Mark as having distinctly declared, that "the Sabbath was made for man, and not man for the Sabbath." It was designed and adapted to promote alike the holiness and the comfort of men; and therefore permitted, and even required, those acts which were needful to renew and preserve the vigor and health of their bodies, that they might the more fully and faithfully worship and serve God, and do good to man on His holy day with all the powers of their souls. Therefore, in His own words, if they had known what this meaneth, "I will have mercy and not sacrifice," they would not have condemned the guiltless.

The declaration that the Son of man is Lord of the Sabbath day, also implies, that Christ, the Son of man, came not to destroy, but to fulfil the law of the Sabbath. This law is clearly contained in the fourth commandment of the moral law, given by Jehovah to Moses amid the solemn scenes of Mount Sinai. Of this, Jesus said, "Heaven and earth shall pass away; but one jot or tittle shall in no wise pass from the law, until all shall be fulfilled." Unless it can be shown that this particular command of the law, "Remember the Sabbath day to keep it holy," has been clearly repealed and annulled by the Saviour in His Gospel, it is still binding on all who believe in His name. But this cannot be shown. So far from this, it seems evident from the whole tenor of His words to the Jews, at various times, respecting the Sabbath, that He always spoke of it as an institution which was ever to continue under the gospel, as it had done under the law. He corrected their superstitious and self-righteous errors respecting it; but, in doing this, He always implied that it must continue to be kept in its true spirit.

We may apply to His declaration, that He is Lord even of the Sabbath day, the same principle of reasoning which He also applied to His Own citation from the Old Testament respecting the resurrection from the dead, saying, "Touching the resurrection from the dead, have ye not read that which was spoken unto you by God, saying, 'I am the God of Abraham, and the God of Isaac, and the God of Jacob?' God is not the God of of the dead, but of the living." So here we may say, that, as it is directly affirmed by our Lord, that He came not to destroy the law, but to fulfil it, and as the keeping of the Sabbath is a commandment of the law, — when Jesus declares that the Son of man is Lord also of the Sabbath day, He is Lord not of a dead, but of a living day. In correcting and reproving the false ideas of the Pharisees respecting it, He only restored it from the letter which killeth to the spirit that giveth life, causing the ministration written and engraven in stones, which was glorious, to have no glory by reason of the glory that excelleth.

On the same principle, we may say,—what some of the most pious and learned commentators on the text have said,—that the declaration may have been designed by our Lord as a prophetic intimation of the fact, that the Gospel was, in its process of magnifying the law of God and making it honorable, to change the seventh-day Sabbath of the law, into the first-day Sabbath of the gospel,—called repeatedly the first day of the week, and, in the book of the Revelation of John, "the Lord's day." Possibly, if not probably, this was intimated by David in the 118th Psalm, the versification of which by Dr. Watts, we often sing in our worship of God: "This is the day which the Lord hath made; we will rejoice and be glad in it."

We say, then, in great confidence, that, if any one will take the facts stated in the Bible respecting the Sabbath day; if he will take the fact that the keeping of it is directly commanded in the moral law of God; that Jesus declared repeatedly, in the Gospel, that this law shall never pass away; and His apostle, that we do not make void the law through faith, but establish the law; that in all our Saviour's instructions respecting the Sabbath, exposing and correcting Jewish errors respecting it, He never intimated, in a single instance, that it was not then binding upon men; that He declared Himself, as the Son of man, to be Lord of the Sabbath, and that it was made for man; that the disciples and first Christians, after His death and resurrection, evidently paid marked attention to the first day of the week; that He Himself first met with them on that day, after He rose from the dead; that they also met on that day to break bread, or, as we have the best reasons to believe, partake of the Lord's Supper; that Paul preached to them on that day; that he afterwards directed the members of the Church in Corinth each to lay by on that day, as God had prospered him, a portion of his earthly possessions for the necessities of the saints, and to aid in advancing the gospel; and that the last of the apostles, John, — " the disciple whom Jesus loved," — wrote, in recording the last words of His

Lord to all His Churches in all ages to the end of time, that he was in the Spirit on the Lord's day, and that the Lord appeared to him in a special manner then, and gave him special messages to deliver to the Churches, — when we place all these interesting and remarkable facts together, and draw from them the general rule which a fair comparison of them with one another seems clearly to demand, — the satisfactory conclusion must be, that the Sabbath is now binding on all men, and on every man, to be remembered and kept holy as a commandment of the moral law of God, which shall never pass away; that Jesus, the Son of man, is Lord of the day; and that He has exercised His lordship, not by annulling it, but, by giving to men, in His own person, and through the practice of His apostles, a larger and more intelligent liberty respecting the manner of keeping it; but no license to desecrate and neglect it. He has shown that the precise day on which a seventh portion of time shall be hallowed in the special worship of God, and the learning and doing of His will, is not important in the spirit of a true obedience to His commandment, as it is made impossible for all men, in all places, from the daily revolutions of the earth upon its axis in its orbit round the sun. He has, therefore, by leading His disciples to keep the first, instead of the seventh day of the week, enlarged and not contracted the blessedness and power of the motives for keeping it holy by making it commemorate the finishing of the work of redemption, as well as the work of the natural creation. And He, therefore, by His Holy Spirit, led an apostle to teach men, in the liberty of the gospel, to rise above, and be superior to those self-complacent and contracted reasonings of the Jews, which, making the precise time, in which it must be kept, essential, fell into the error rebuked in the Epistle to the Colossians: "Let no man, therefore, judge you in meat, or in drink, or in respect of an holy day, or of the new moon, or of the Sabbath days: which are a shadow of things to come; but the body is Christ," — Paul thus agreeing, in the teachings of his Epistle, with the remarkable declaration of Jesus, that "the Son of man is Lord, even of the Sabbath day."

Of this, as we think, very strong evidence from the Bible of the binding obligation of the law of the Sabbath, as a moral, and not a positive or temporary, institution, under the Gospel of Christ, there are two facts, one of a historical, and the other of a natural or physiological kind, strongly corroborative.

The historical fact is, that from the earliest history of the Christian Churches, the first day of the week has been reverenced by being devoted, as the Lord's day, to be a Sabbath or day of rest from the earthly toils of other days, and passed in the worship and enjoyment of God in Christ.

And the natural or physiological fact is, that the direct testimony of a great number of the most learned and impartial men, sought and given with direct reference to this subject,—testimony thus given by statesmen, physicians, lawyers, machinists, merchants, and intelligent men from other departments of life,—agrees in affirming, that man and beast most evidently need the rest and recreation of one day in seven, for the restoration and vigor of their health and energy, otherwise exhausted by the perpetual toils and cares of life.

To this it may be added, that when the deistical philosophers, in a nominally Christian nation, not yet a century ago, attempted to abolish the Christian Sabbath, they were so deeply convinced of the natural need of men of some similar institution, that they appointed one day in ten as a season for similar needed rest and recreation, and change of employment, — thus bearing their unwilling testimony to the truth that the Sabbath was made for man.

II. With these evidences, then, of its Divine authority, as it is confirmed by the precepts and practice of Jesus and His apostles, and the history of all the Churches of Christ, we are prepared to consider the duty of its " more strict observance."

This implies that its observance among us has been, and is, too greatly neglected, and needs to be more strict. Need I go into details to show that this is true? Is it not evident to every serious observer of the habits of our country and commonwealth and city, that the neglect of the worship of God on the Sabbath, and the positive and unnecessary breaking of its rest, by various practices, has of late years greatly increased?

In our own city and vicinity we are certainly

coming very near, under fair and plausible names, to theatrical performances on the evening of the Lord's day; to political harangues during the day and evening, sometimes from the lips of professed preachers of the Gospel; to habitual drives for pleasure; and a great neglect of attendance on the public worship of God, and the hearing of His Word, by private persons.

Without speaking farther of what all know, let us inquire what we ought to do for the more strict observance of the day.

To this inquiry it may be said, generally, that, as it is a day of rest on earth, in which men may, in the use of its means, be preparing to enter into the rest of heaven, and as they are specially encouraged and aided by the day to come unto Christ, the Lord of the Sabbath, and find "rest unto their souls," which shall thus prepare them for rest eternal; so, whatever duties lead them most directly and perfectly to rest in Christ must be, so far as practicable, done; and all acts which hinder them from thus coming unto Him, and finding rest unto their souls, on this day of rest, ought to be, so far as practicable, avoided.

In doing these duties, and abstaining from these unnecessary practices, we are ever to keep in mind that the Gospel teaches us that we are in a world of discipline; in which, for our highest good, we are to be continually tried, in our characters and conduct, by questions respecting truth and duty. On this account our path is not, and ought not to be, always and clearly "chalked out for us." Good is not to be done altogether or mainly by law, but by the Gospel. Some men among us are always relying on law too much. They would, in this sense, go back to the "weak and beggarly elements of this world," by specifying in distinct rules what may be done or left undone respecting the forms and institutions of religion,— and, of course, in regard to the keeping of the Sabbath,— instead of leaving the conduct to be prompted and governed by the intelligence of Christian love. The tendency of such legal action, respecting Christian duty, is to make the manners of men stiff, and suspicious, and censorious; not free, natural, confiding, kind and charitable.

We are ever to remember, that, in respect to all the forms and institutions of religion, we "have been called unto liberty; only we should use not our liberty as an occasion to the flesh, but by love serve one another." In regard to the keeping of the Sabbath, therefore, we are to feel, and act as if we felt, that we are "not under law, but under grace." We are to keep it, from the promptings of supreme love, and ever-operative gratitude and praise to God, in Christ; regarding it not as a yoke, but as a privilege; and well assured that when men are under the influence of the love and service of Jesus, they need not fear that they shall not arrive at clear and satisfactory views of truth and duty, respecting the keeping of the Lord's day.

There ought to be among us a more strict observance of the Sabbath, under the influence of this love and liberty of the Gospel, in our *public, social, domestic,* and *personal* duties respecting it.

By our PUBLIC duties respecting it, I would be understood to mean the influence we may properly exert on the acts of the government under which we live. It is plain that for its acts, each of us, as a subject of it, can be only indirectly and partly accountable. And this, our accountability, must be proportioned to the degree of influence we can exert in directing its action. This is, in most cases, small in degree, and very limited in extent. To whatever degree and extent it can be effectual, we are accountable, and no farther. But, to that degree and extent, we ought to exert our influence in promoting the public keeping of the Lord's day.

By the truths we embrace, and strive to promote respecting it; by our personal example in keeping it; by the character of the persons we aid in placing in positions of public trust, — we can, and ought to strive to, promote its public observance. After having faithfully made such efforts, our personal accountability for what may be done by government, ceases. But whatever influence we can wield ought to be used to the extent of our ability.

In this way the Churches of Christian disciples, and private believers in Jesus, as they increase in numbers and influence in a nation, shall gradually, but surely make the government what the people are; and gradually, but surely, the rulers, of whatever form the government may be, whether despotic or democratic, shall be eventually wise men, ruling in the fear of the Lord, keeping His Sabbaths and reverencing His sanctuary, knowing that He is the Lord. In our own government does not much need to be done, in such ways, to promote the better observance of this holy time?

It is thus, also, with regard to our SOCIAL duties in keeping the Sabbath. In these I would include particularly the acts of the city, or town, or village, in which each of us may reside; and the various circles, whether of organized associations, or of a smaller kind, with which individuals may be connected. In these, much more efficaciously than in any departments of the public government, each person may exert an influence for good. In any official position he may hold, either permanently, or only for a limited time, each private disciple can, in many ways, directly or indirectly, by his word, his acts, his example, do much to promote the observance of God's Sabbath, and the reverence of His sanctuary. This may be done, in any such bodies as are formed to advance public ends and private interests, like manufacturing companies, or railroad and steamboat associations. In any of those combinations of men where the personal influence, or the vote of an individual, can be intelligently and wisely used, to promote the keeping of the Sabbath, it ought, in conformity with the principles of the Gospel already stated, to be done.

I say, on the principles of the Gospel already stated, meaning by this, those principles which show us that we are under a dispensation of things, in a world of trial, where questions of truth and duty often arise in which it is difficult to decide what course of action, respecting the keeping of His Sabbaths, may be most pleasing to God, and, therefore, of the highest benefit to man.

Whatever may be the decisions of a truly Christian wisdom on such subjects, what I wish to say is this: that all who would keep the Sabbath socially, in the light and liberty of the Gospel, must be prepared to find questions of religious duty sometimes arising, which call not for quick and rash decisions, and stringent laws, but for humble, patient, prayerful watchfulness; and a firmer reliance on the ultimate influence of Christian faith, working by love, in men, than on laws quickly enacted, and sternly enforced. God will have mercy, and not sacrifice. We must have moral courage enough to be kind and forbearing and long-suffering to man in all our zeal for God.

In our DOMESTIC relations,—by which are meant those of the family-circle,—in our respective households, the influence, good or bad, of every member, in regard to the Sabbath, is most directly exerted by one's self, and felt by others. To this, therefore, the fourth commandment of the law of God directly refers, and is now binding: "In it thou shalt not do any work; thou, nor *thy son*, nor *thy daughter*, nor thy *man-servant*, nor thy *maid-servant*, nor thy *cattle*, nor thy *stranger* that is within thy gates." Regard should be had, in all domestic arrangements, to the religious good and bodily rest of servants.

How interesting and instructive it is, thus to have the law of God magnified and made honorable, as it is, by the Gospel, entering, by faith in Christ, our families, and commanding us, in the name of the Lord of the Sabbath day, to keep it holy; thus blessing all the families of the earth by its sacred rest; in which the parents and children, one day in every seven, take sweet counsel in their home, and go to the house of God in company. What a fountain of purity and peace is thus opened, by the arrangement of God, in every household, from which streams of blessed influence shall flow out into all the masses of a nation, and make glad the city of God. "Happy is that people that is in such a case: yea, happy is that people whose God is the Lord."

In our PERSONAL and private habits, ought there not to be a more strict observance of the Sabbath? In our time of rising in the morning; in the kind of books we read; in the nature of the thoughts and imaginations we indulge; in the regularity and number of the times in which we attend the public worship of God; in the kind of silent, yet great influence we thus exert on all whom we love in our domestic circle, ought there not to be more faithfulness? In prayer to God, and the searching of the Scriptures, ought not each of us to be more faithful, fervent, diligent? Should we not avoid the tendency to indolence, in which, during its hours, we may be tempted to indulge?

There are several very important, practical inferences, which might, were there time, be drawn from this subject, as thus presented.

One of them, were I to attempt to speak of them, would be the evidence it gives of the Divine nature and authority of Jesus. He is Lord even of the Sabbath day, which day we are commanded to remember and keep holy, in God's eternal law.

But let me only speak, in closing, of the blessed opportunity afforded to every person, in a Christian land, by the weekly recurrence of each Sabbath, for coming unto Jesus, the Lord of the Sabbath, and finding rest unto the soul! Possibly, it might be said, with truth, that our Lord's frequent cures of the maladies of men, when He was on earth, on the Sabbath day, were designed to direct our attention to this blessed truth. On this day He healed the man with the withered hand; on this day He loosed the woman who "had a spirit of infirmity eighteen years, and was bowed together, and could in no wise lift up herself;" on this day He commanded the man who had been waiting a long time at the pool of Bethesda, and had an infirmity thirty and eight years, to rise, take up his bed, and walk; and immediately he was made whole, and took up his bed and walked. "And on the same day was the Sabbath."

It was on the Sabbath day that Jesus made clay, and opened the eyes of the man who was blind from his birth. It was on the Sabbath day that He went into the synagogue, in Nazareth, where He had been brought up, and "stood up for to read;" and when He had opened the book He found the place where it is written, "The Spirit of the Lord is upon me, because he hath anointed me to preach the Gospel to the poor; He hath sent me to heal the broken-hearted, to preach deliverance to the captives, and recovering of sight to the blind; to set at liberty them that are bruised; to preach the acceptable year of the Lord." "And He began to say unto them, 'This day is this Scripture fulfilled in your ears.'"

So now, in our time, He comes by His Word, His preachers, His Spirit, in the rest of every Sabbath day, of which He *is* the Lord, to heal the diseases of the souls of men; to cause the spiritually blind to see, the deaf to hear, the lame to walk; to heal the broken-hearted; to deliver men from the slavery of sin; to set at liberty them that are bruised; to preach the acceptable year of the Lord.

BY THE
CONGREGATIONAL PASTORS OF BOSTON,

RECOMMENDED BY THE

Boston Congregational Council.

The following are now published, and ready for delivery:—

No. 1 THE RESULT OF COUNCIL Complete.

No. 2 THE CHRISTIAN'S RECONSECRATION. By Rev. E. K. ALDEN, Pastor of Phillips Church

No. 3. THE WORLDLINESS OF NOMINAL CHRISTIANS. By Rev. Dr. WEBB, Pastor of Shawmut Church.

No. 4 THE DUTY OF CHRISTIANS TO UNITE WITH SOME CHURCH, AND THE DUTY OF CHURCH-MEMBERS TO UNITE WITH THE CHURCH WHERE THEY STATEDLY WORSHIP By Rev. S P. FAY, Pastor of Salem Church.

No. 5. THE DUTY OF DAILY SECRET PRAYER and DAILY STUDY OF THE BIBLE. By Rev. J. M MANNING.

No. 6. REVIVALS OF RELIGION. By Rev. J. E TODD

No. 7. THE DIVINE SOVEREIGNTY IN ITS RELATION TO HUMAN SALVATION. By Rev. Mr. BAKER.

No. 8. THE DUTY OF A MORE STRICT OBSERVANCE OF THE SABBATH. By Rev. Dr. BLAGDEN.

The remaining Addresses will follow at intervals of about one week viz:—

THE SPREAD OF THE GOSPEL IN THE CITY AMONG THE POOR, AND THOSE WHO HABITUALLY NEGLECT THE SERVICES OF THE SABBATH. By Rev. Dr DEXTER

THE CHRISTIAN'S DUTY TO WORK FOR THE SAVING OF SOULS. By Rev. Mr. BINGHAM.

THE POWER AND OFFICE OF THE HOLY SPIRIT. By Rev. Dr. ADAMS.

THE POWER OF PRAYER. By Rev. Dr KIRK.

No. 9. Published by direction of the Congregational Churches of Boston.

THE
POWER OF PRAYER.

BY

REV. E. N. KIRK, D.D.

BOSTON:
NICHOLS AND NOYES.
1866.

THE

POWER OF PRAYER.

BY

Rev. E. N. KIRK, D.D.

BOSTON:
NICHOLS AND NOYES.
1866.

Entered according to Act of Congress, in the year 1866, by

NICHOLS AND NOYES,

In the Clerk's Office of the District Court of the District of Massachusetts.

CAMBRIDGE:
STEREOTYPED AND PRINTED BY JOHN WILSON AND SONS.

THE POWER OF PRAYER.

In nothing is the world more opposed to Christ than in His revelation of mysteries to be believed and acted on in daily life. And when a worldly person embraces His religion in name merely, as is frequently done, the very first step is to strip it of mysteries and reduce it to a philosophy or a science, to something that can be seen by the eyes, or demonstrated to the understanding, and thus relieve him of the inconvenience of appearing unreasonable to other worldly persons. Faith, or the belief of that which "eye hath not seen, nor ear heard, nor hath entered into the heart of man" by invention or discovery, — the world utterly discards.

Prominent among the mysteries of the Gospel is Prayer; not so much when considered as adoration, confession, thanksgiving, or even supplication; not at all, when considered as a direct means of refining our own hearts; but as a POWER, a power over God; that is the mystery in which faith believes.

Considered as a privilege, prayer is wonderful; but as a force, it transcends all our earthly wisdom, and can be recognized by Faith alone. We see, for instance, the man Moses staying the arm of Omnipotence just uplifted to strike down a guilty race, as described in Numbers xiv. 11. Was it science, or statesmanship, or military prowess, poetic talent or eloquence, that saved that people? No, it was the power of prayer. "And the Lord said, I have pardoned according to *thy word.*"

We see Abraham pleading for the people of Sodom, and reducing, step by step, the conditions of their salvation to narrower and easier terms.

We see Elijah, a man like ourselves, shutting the windows of heaven for more than three years; then, bowed on Carmel, controlling the forces of nature simply by the power of prayer, and bringing down the rain that saved a nation from destruction.

Read the record of David's experience, in his

Psalms. Hearken to that voice of pleading which comes down to us from the early ages, and observe the soul putting forth the energy of faith successfully; "Make haste to help me: innumerable evils have compassed me: be pleased, O Lord! to deliver me; Be not silent to me, lest I become like them that go down to the pit." Indeed, the Psalms very frequently are a record of prayer for personal deliverance; almost uniformly ending with a grateful record of the answer given to each petition. They are monuments of the power of prayer. Nay, it is remarkable that there is scarcely one definite prayer recorded, the answer to which is not equally registered.

Esther, Daniel, Gideon, Samuel, Nehemiah, Hezekiah, and many others, are described as having, like Jacob, "power with God."

This view of prayer was frequently presented by our Saviour in His instructions. Notice these words in Luke xi. 9, "Ask," "seek," "knock," in their connection, and you see that they are climactic; indicating increasing earnestness and importunity. The hour is late: the family are in bed. The man does not rise for a simple request from his friend. He even presents reasons against rising. But, at length, the Lord says, it is "importunity" that makes him yield. The same object He had in view in the parable of the widow; the judge yielded to nothing but her importunity: "He spake a parable unto them to this end, that men ought always to pray and not faint." And what is it makes them tend to faint, but God's long delay, and that resistance by which He tests their faith? Jacob was resisted. The woman of Syrophenicia was resisted: the widow before the judge was resisted: the friend was at first refused, and reasons were given for not granting his request. The faithful student of Scripture cannot fail to mark that these are illustrations of one kind or degree of prayer.

The immediate measure introducing the Christian dispensation was, by the Lord's direct orders, a protracted prayer-meeting.

Peter was released from prison by the prayers of the Church. James declared that the prayer of faith should save the sick.

These instances are sufficient to show that the Scriptures reveal the power of prayer; declaring that man by believing prayer has power over the weather, over the angels, over diseases, over God Himself, within defined limits.

But many refuse to believe this principle on either of the two grounds, God's testimony or man's experience. They require what is to them more authoritative and conclusive, a philosophical explanation *why* and *how* God is moved by prayer. This, however, is to abandon the sphere of faith and the supernatural. Semi-rationalists admit that prayer benefits the suppliant directly, but its power over God they deny. Supposing themselves to be believers, they have only the faith of science; not that of either ordinary life or religion. They adopt the false principle in this matter, of believing only what they can explain; which should make them atheists, for they do not know how or why God exists. We may perplex our minds with a host of objections and difficulties about an unoriginated, infinite life and personality; still, faith believes there is such a life and personality. Pure rationalism must be atheistic.

He that waits to pray until he can discover reasons and explanations full and satisfactory why and how man has power with his Creator will probably never exercise that power. He that counts for nothing the teachings, testimony, and promises of God's word cannot pray in faith or "in the Holy Ghost." (Jude 20.)

This is a vital point in the Christian religion. If the strong men of prayer, like Moses, Elijah, David, Daniel, and Paul, especially if the woman of Syrophenicia, had withheld their belief in the efficacy of prayer until they had made a logical argument proving it, we should never have had the history of their glorious achievements. The roll of honor, in the eleventh chapter of Hebrews, had never been written, if the illustrious men it commends had been rationalists.

If any one insists that God is unchangeable in such a sense that our suffering and supplication do not affect both His sensibilities and His will, we refer them to the earthly life of Him who, as Son of man, took our places and undertook our cause.

There they may discover in His redemptive work the most conclusive and most impressive exhibition of importunity and its power with God, the most complete overthrowing of the objections to importunate prayer. Two branches of it had "power with God" even more than with men,— the Atonement and Prayer. Why could not God forgive us, as a kind Father, without the intervention of the humiliating incarnation of His Son; the life of the "Man of sorrows;" the scenes of the garden, and the hill of Golgotha? Proud Reason, take off thy shoes here, for the ground is holy. The sacrifice of Jesus is the indispensable medium of our salvation. Why did the Father exact it? Whether we can answer it or not, the fact remains,—"He spared not His Son," even for His "crying."

Then turn to His praying. He surely found it necessary to be importunate. Sweating as it were great drops of blood, thrice He fell upon His face, crying for release from the cup of anguish. "He offered up prayer and supplication with strong crying and tears." "And, being in an agony, He prayed more earnestly." Why may not the same necessity be laid on them who are made one with Him, called to bear His cross, and drink His cup, and follow Him, "filling up what is behind of the sufferings of Christ"?

Why may not there be in the Divine nature a

demand for more than mere desire on the part of him who would secure the exercise of Divine mercy toward sinners? No one can intelligently affirm that there is not.

Brethren, believe the word of God when it declares, "Ask, and ye shall receive." If you can discover *why* you shall receive, it is very well. But do not wait for that. "Believe; for all things are possible to him that believeth."

Guard against that spirit which saturates the very atmosphere of this metropolis, the spirit that demands stronger reasons for believing any proposition than that it is founded upon the testimony of the Bible. The moment you yield to it, you have crossed over the line that separates the kingdom of Christ from the world. Take your position either as an unbeliever, and say, "I believe only what I can prove;" or as a believer, and say, "I believe the words of Christ as recorded in the Scriptures."

If any one affirms that prayer, and especially importunate prayer, is dictating to God, tell him it is no more so than planting grain; for He has ordained both to be the immediate means of securing certain desired results. If any one asks you whether any person can obtain any thing he wants by praying for it, reply to him, that this is not implied in the Scriptural view of prayer, or any Scriptural promise. There are limitations and conditions and relations of prevailing prayer which guard it against such an absurdity.

If any one inquires how we can reconcile the promises of answer to the prayer of faith, with the fact that the children of believing parents have died in impenitence, we certainly have a right to reply, You do not know that those parents ever prayed according to God's requirements.

"But," it may then be replied, "this makes it always uncertain to any person, because he is not sure he has complied with all the conditions of the promises." To this we answer, The case is exactly parallel with that of salvation itself. To low degrees of faith, uncertainty of the result is always attached. Faith, in its higher exercise, alone can bring certainty.

Others have asked, if the warnings against using "vain repetitions" do not meet this case. By no means. Vain repetitions are words used as charms, of which so many specimens may be found in the various superstitions of the world.

Others find a difficulty in this passage, "Your heavenly Father knoweth of what things ye have need before ye ask." "Why, then, pray and importune?" they say. Our first reply is, that whether we can answer this inquiry or not, we can safely affirm, that it was not designed to discourage, but to encourage prayer. Our second reply is, in the language of another, "Superstition places the reason of the hearing of prayer not in the grace of God, but in its own godless work. Unbelief deduces the uselessness of prayer from the omniscience of God, in Whom it does not itself believe. Faith rests its poor prayer precisely on this holy, gracious, Divine knowledge. Thus our Lord teaches us to pray in faith *because* God knows, before the petition, what we need; and, consequently, can Himself prompt the acceptable prayer, and fulfil it accordingly. These words of the Saviour are to be taken as the reason which prevents the Christian from praying after the heathen manner." (Olshausen *in loc.*) If God were not acquainted with all our wants, He could not command our adoration or confidence.

What, then, are—

THE ELEMENTS OF PREVAILING PRAYER?

1. *Faith.* "He that cometh to God must believe" two propositions: ".that God is, and that He is the Rewarder of them who diligently seek Him."

In other words, he must believe in the power of prayer; that if he diligently and properly seeks of God a certain blessing, he will get it, so far as that blessing lies within the scope of express promise. Look at the Syrophenician woman's wonderful prayer: she definitely expected to be answered. Nothing daunted or discouraged her, though her faith was put to the severest tests. Yet this woman had nothing but the promise furnished by the Saviour's character and disposition, for it was understood in her day that His personal mission was to the Jews alone.

We have what she knew nothing of,— the name of Christ as our plea. We know that He has removed every barrier from our way to the mercy-seat. And we know that the promises of God to us are all "in Him, yea and amen,"— promises covering every point of human necessity. Some of these are unconditional and general. We say "unconditional," and yet not one of them will be fulfilled but in answer to prayer, not even that which declares that Christ will subdue the world to Himself. There are other promises directly and wholly conditioned on prayer. When, therefore, we have prayed for the objects they contain, we must expect them. Some are limited by other conditions. Expectation of their fulfilment, in cases where such conditions are not complied with, is not faith, but presumption; like the expectations of those who look for heaven without meeting the requirements of the Gospel. Then again, we must not fix a time or a mode of answering a prayer where God has not; but "hope against hope," and place promises against providences.

But God is honored by a faith that expects His actions ultimately, whatever He may be doing at present, to be as good and gracious as His word, and a fulfilment of them; a faith which believes He is able, willing, and desirous to do all He has promised to do.

2. *Intense desire is an element of the higher grade of prayer.* This the Saviour indicated

when He remarked concerning demons, that His disciples had not faith to exorcise them,—"this kind goeth not out but by fasting and prayer." Ordinary desire is here not sufficiently strong. Ordinary prayer is here unavailing. That woman of Canaan had probably endured a long trial with her daughter. Night and day, the child's agony had racked her spirit. And now she comes to pour out the grief of months, perhaps of years, in one gushing prayer. And she could afford to spend that precious moment on nothing else,—"Lord, my daughter is grievously vexed with a devil."

Some good men have been averse to the representation of prayer as an expression of intense desire, even to agony. But they surely have overlooked the history of Jacob, of Hannah, of Mordecai, of Hezekiah, of Paul, nay, of the Lord Himself, who offered up prayer "with strong crying and tears." Do these brethren deny that we are permitted in this very matter to "fill up what is behind of the sufferings of Christ"? If He is not our pattern in praying, in what respects are we to imitate Him?

And, if we come down from this height, we

shall find that, in every subsequent age, the most eminent of His servants have been distinguished for intense desires for His glory, and for their own spiritual good, and the salvation of others.

This importunate prayer makes the crisis in the history of almost every converted soul. To cite thousands of instances would be easy. Augustine, Brainerd, Whitfield, came into the kingdom of God in the agony of prayer. Then, every great revival of religion that has blessed our world, every great stage in the advance of the kingdom of Christ, has been preceded, not by gentle requests merely, but by what has properly been called the agony of prayer. Such was the case when the captive Church was released and returned to Palestine, in answer to the prayer of Daniel and Nehemiah. It was so in the Reformation that blessed our world in the sixteenth century.

Of the many modern specimens of the power of prayer, I present one instance in which the challenge was made by scepticism to faith. The Rev. A. B. Earle was preaching in Oneonta, N.Y., about the year 1850. He had insisted strongly in his discourse, one day, on the efficacy of earnest, determined, persevering prayer in securing the conversion of men. At the close of the sermon, Mr. Otis — a lawyer, a notorious sceptic, who had confirmed many in his own views — arose, and addressed the preacher with this remark, " Mr. Earle, I do not believe a word of the doctrine you have been asserting. Now, if you wish to try it on a hard case, try it on me." The preacher replied, " Mr. Otis, come forward here, and present yourself as asking the prayers of God's people." He refused to come.

The preacher then requested all the Church to retire to their closets at a specified hour, — and begged him to remember the hour, — in which they should pray specially for his conversion. In the course of the third day from that, he arose in the midst of the congregation, and said, " I may as well break the ice now as at any time; I wish somebody to pray for me." Mr. Earle then said, " Will you come to this front seat that we may pray for you?" He replied, "Anywhere, if some one will pray for me." He came forward: and, kneeling, he filled the house with his sobs. To-day he is preaching, in the ranks of the Methodist ministry, that Gospel he once despised.

If the full history of the recent Rebellion could be written, we cannot entertain a doubt, that the world would see that, even more gloriously than the patriotism and skill and material resources of the government and people, the power of prayer is set forth by it. If ever a President was remembered in prayer, Mr. Lincoln was. If ever earnest, intense prayer ascended to heaven, it was from April, 1861, to April, 1865, for the life of this nation.

3. *Patient importunity is another characteristic of powerful or prevailing prayer.* It is remarkable that a man of such gigantic intellect as Samuel Taylor Coleridge, misled by the speculations of German philosophers, should yet have had such views of the grandeur, solemnity, and power of earnest prayer as at once bringing the greatest blessings to the earth, and most profoundly taxing the sensibilities of the heart. He once made this remark to De Quincey: "Prayer with the whole soul is the highest

energy of which the human heart is capable; and therefore the great mass of worldly men are absolutely incapable of prayer."

Long afterward he said to his nephew: " I have no difficulty in [believing in] forgiveness. Neither do I find or reckon most solemn faith in God, as a real object, the most arduous act of reason and will. Oh no! it is *to pray*, to pray as God would have us: this is what at times makes me turn cold to my soul. Believe me, to pray with all your heart and strength, with the reason and the will; to believe vividly that God will listen to your voice through Christ, and verily do the thing He pleaseth thereupon, — this is the last, the greatest achievement of a Christian's warfare on earth." And then, bursting into tears, he begged his nephew to pray for him.

Yes, brethren, this is the great truth the Church needs now to comprehend to achieve her final victory. "This kind goeth not out but by fasting and prayer;" there are demons commanding the strongholds of the world that can be cast out only by the highest kind of prayer.

We have not outlived the Old Testament. There we have, among others, this striking exhibition of the power of importunate prayer. There we see that God sometimes offers resistance to the suppliant, and yet yields to importunity, as in the case of Abraham's grandson whose birth-name was Jacob, afterward changed to Israel. There certainly has been too little made of his remarkable experience, and of that name by which he was finally known, by which the ancient people of God were known, and which has been transferred to the Church of the new dispensation.

Let us recall the meaning of that new title; and the circumstances in view of which it was conferred. Israel is a Heaven-chosen, Heaven-imparted name. The man who bore it was at his birth called Jacob, from the prophetic action he then performed of seizing his twin-brother by the heel; and the name in the Hebrew tongue is equivalent to Supplanter.

Out of his basely supplanting Esau came the miseries of his youth and early manhood. But out of the wonderful faith he manifested when those miseries were culminating at the ford Jabbok, came the new name Israel.

Returning from the north with his large family, his flocks and herds, he was informed, as he approached the Jordan, that the outraged Esau was coming to meet him.

Weak, from the sense of his own unfairness toward his brother, aware of his inability to make a military defence, he adopted the only two measures left to him: a judicious attempt to appease his brother, and an appeal to the God of Abraham. Of the first we need not now speak, as our attention is here turned to the most mysterious feature of prayer; that is, its power as exhibited in this man.

And we must first be assured that this mysterious wrestling with the angel was prayer; of which we are made sure by several statements in the Scriptures. The first is, that Jacob was seeking a blessing. His language, "Deliver me, I pray Thee, from my brother," "I will not let Thee go, except Thou bless me," expresses his object in struggling. And again, "The angel," it is said, "blessed him there." And then again, the prophet Hosea (xii. 3, 4) distinctly states that "he made supplication unto" God.

The question then arises, Was the angel the Son of God, the Jehovah of the Old Testament? This is equally determined by the Word of God.

Jacob would not have asked a mere angel to change Esau's vengeful heart; for that was manifestly the blessing he sought and obtained. Again, he is said to have had "power with God" in this contest. And he declares he had seen God face to face in it. Then Hosea makes the angel and God identical: "He had power with God; yea, he had power over the angel, and prevailed."

The next point of interest in this wonderful story is, that God resisted Jacob. That was the intention of His assuming the attitude of a wrestler, holding Jacob all night in the contest, laming his thigh, and at length asking to be released from his grasp.

On this point we must dwell a moment, for the sake of those who are averse to this view of prayer.

Their reasoning, like much other, contradicts the Scriptures, and the experience of the most eminent children of God. It contradicts the word of God. Jacob did not get the blessing for simply asking: he wrestled all night. And God, so far from censuring him for it, gave him the blessing because of his importunity; He removed the old name " Supplanter," and gave him a new name, Prince of God. And that name Israel has now become the permanent title of the Church of God. We are not Jacobites, but Israelites; not supplanters, but a race having " power with God and men" by the importunity of believing prayer. The prayer of Hannah was a long-continued, weeping prayer. The prayer of the prophet Jonah was a prayer of anguish uttered, as he expressed it, out of "the belly of hell:" "I cried by reason of my affliction unto the Lord, and He heard me."

4. *Humility.* As we see it illustrated in the woman of Syrophenicia. At first the Lord appeared to neglect her. Then He reasoned with the disciples against her petitions. Then He reasoned more directly to her against it, and added to this a wound through her national feelings. But all the time her soul was poised and collected in the strength of meekness. She manifested none of the impatience, the sensitiveness, or the exacting spirit, of pride. She recognized herself to be purely a suppliant, and the Saviour to be the Master of His own power and

possessions. He might choose His own time and way of bestowing His gifts. This agrees with intense earnestness, and is indispensable to prevailing with God.

5. *Obedience.* The spirit of entire submission to God's will; the determination to do whatever He makes it manifest He would have us do. If we ask for a revival of religion, and have not given up our choice and determination of the way in which it shall come, and the kind and amount of labor we are to perform, we cannot reasonably expect to prevail with God. " Obedience is better than sacrifice " in His sight. We may omit the words in importunate prayer; but we must never omit the sentiment and purpose they express : " Thy will be done."

If you are seeking the conversion of your children, you must give up your will about their worldly interests, and the way in which God shall convert them, saying, " Not my will, but Thine be done."

Brethren, our work is before us ; the most important portion of which is prayer. If we want power with God like Jacob, we must pray like him. If we want spiritual power with men, we must pray like him. The language of our hearts must be, "I will not let Thee go except Thou bless me." There are tithes of importunate prayer yet to be brought into the Lord's storehouse, before He will "open the windows of heaven, and pour out a blessing that there shall not be room enough to receive it."

Who are Israel's descendants? They are the Princes of God, who have "power with God and with man," and have "prevailed" in prayer. As such they will be known in heaven.

And for what have we come to such a time as this, if not to call forth that mightiest of human agencies, to exert the power of prayer to its utmost extent? Our city calls for it. Our country calls for it. Prayer can reconstruct this country; not without statesmanship, but by making it wise and efficient, by subduing passion and prejudice, and attaching the hearts of the entire people to the government, and to one another.

The Church demands it: perishing souls demand it. Let us pray "the prayer of faith," "the fervent, effectual prayer of a righteous man, that availeth much," that has power with God and with men. For our own sakes let us covet the blessedness of partaking with our blessed Lord, in so far as it be assigned to us, of those sufferings "which are behind." Surely they must live the nearest to Him who most fully share the sympathy that brought Him to this earth, and the burden-bearing that culminated on the cross.

Let us pray the prayer of faith for the immediate coming of the Lord, not in His body, but by His Holy Spirit, to raise the human race to a higher level, and to bring to pass the saying that is written: "Behold the tabernacle of God is with men, and He will dwell with them."

Addresses to Church Members

BY THE

CONGREGATIONAL PASTORS OF BOSTON,

RECOMMENDED BY THE

Boston Congregational Council.

The following are now published, and ready for delivery: —

No. 1. THE RESULT OF COUNCIL. Complete.

No. 2. THE CHRISTIAN'S RECONSECRATION. By Rev. E. K. ALDEN, Pastor of Phillips Church.

No. 3. THE WORLDLINESS OF NOMINAL CHRISTIANS. By Rev. Dr. WEBB, Pastor of Shawmut Church.

No. 4. THE DUTY OF CHRISTIANS TO UNITE WITH SOME CHURCH, AND THE DUTY OF CHURCH-MEMBERS TO UNITE WITH THE CHURCH WHERE THEY STATEDLY WORSHIP. By Rev. S. P. FAY, Pastor of Salem Church.

No. 5. THE DUTY OF DAILY SECRET PRAYER and DAILY STUDY OF THE BIBLE. By Rev. J. M. MANNING.

No. 6. REVIVALS OF RELIGION. By Rev. J. E. TODD.

No. 7. THE DIVINE SOVEREIGNTY IN ITS RELATION TO HUMAN SALVATION. By Rev. Mr. BAKER.

No. 8. THE DUTY OF A MORE STRICT OBSERVANCE OF THE SABBATH. By Rev. Dr. BLAGDEN.

No. 9. THE POWER OF PRAYER. By Rev. Dr. KIRK.

The remaining Addresses will follow at intervals of about one week; viz: —

THE SPREAD OF THE GOSPEL IN THE CITY AMONG THE POOR, AND THOSE WHO HABITUALLY NEGLECT THE SERVICES OF THE SABBATH. By Rev. Dr. DEXTER.

THE CHRISTIAN'S DUTY TO WORK FOR THE SAVING OF SOULS. By Rev. Mr. BINGHAM.

THE POWER AND OFFICE OF THE HOLY SPIRIT. By Rev. Dr. ADAMS.

No. 10. *Published by direction of the Congregational Churches of Boston.*

THE

POWER AND OFFICE

OF

THE HOLY SPIRIT.

BY

Rev. N. ADAMS, D.D.

BOSTON:
NICHOLS AND NOYES.
1866.

THE
POWER AND OFFICE
OF
THE HOLY SPIRIT.

BY

Rev. N. ADAMS, D.D.

BOSTON:
NICHOLS AND NOYES.
1866.

Entered according to Act of Congress, in the year 1866, by

NICHOLS AND NOYES,

In the Clerk's Office of the District Court of the District of Massachusetts.

CAMBRIDGE:
STEREOTYPED AND PRINTED BY JOHN WILSON AND SONS.

THE POWER AND OFFICE OF THE HOLY SPIRIT.

During those tender and endearing moments when the Saviour was preparing the disciples for his own departure, He promised them "another Comforter," who should abide with them for ever. This implies that He himself had been a Comforter. And what a Comforter Jesus is, let the experience of the eleven disciples, and the sorrowing hearts of eighteen centuries, testify. No one epithet can express the fulness of Christ or of the Holy Spirit; yet, of all the words in our tongue proposed as the rendering of this designation of the Holy Spirit by the Saviour, none is more beautiful, more comprehensive, and, on the whole, more just to the original, than the word "Comforter."

"Another Comforter." Progress is the law in the works of God. Another Comforter, therefore, we may be sure would cause the disciples no painful perception of inferiority, or sense of loss. Not many days after, they found themselves, — unlearned and ignorant, men, — addressing people in strange languages. Words spoken by them made converts by thousands, in one day, to the crucified One. Yet this by no means constituted their chief joy. That which happens to one's own soul has an interest for him beyond all outward phenomena. The Great Teacher seems to imply this when He says, " Notwithstanding, in this rejoice not, that the spirits are subject unto you; but rather rejoice because your names are written in heaven." These disciples came, in one hour, to a consciousness of wonderful enlargement in their spiritual perceptions. The whole life of Jesus, especially words and actions of his till then comparatively obscure, were as when the flames of many gas-burners are raised at once by a single motion. Suddenly these men were in a new spiritual world; and the light of it was He of whom, in relation to heaven, it is said, — " the Lamb is the light thereof."

Happy, happy men! conscious of a new spiritual state surpassing in value the mere gift of tongues and influence over a multitude! "They were all filled with the Holy Ghost."

Had the gift of tongues been the chief part of the Holy Spirit's work in the apostles, there would be ground for the apprehension that the excellent greatness in this gift of another Comforter was confined to the early Church. But no; miracles were the least part of His intention,—a mere alphabet in his communications to the objects of his grace.

Not to the first disciples alone, therefore, did the gift of the Comforter appertain. For said Jesus, "Neither pray I for these alone, but for them also which shall believe on me through their word." You, dear Christian friend, are in all respects as truly included in the gift of the Comforter as were the eleven disciples. These pages are designed to assist you in your conceptions of Him. May He guide us into all truth!

WHO IS IT,—who must He be, that is capable of taking up the work of the GOD-MAN and carrying it on to perfection?

To make atonement for sin,—chief as it is

among the works of God,—does not bring into view the same executive attributes which are employed in dealing with human minds, one by one; in adapting the method of recovery to the peculiarities of each; and in carrying on the work of grace through the vicissitudes of personal history. Who must He be that creates successive dispensations of thought among men; controls the wonderful tides of religious feeling; brings on those seasons of wide-spread, irresistible impression concerning things spiritual and eternal; and, at the same time, is conversant with every mood of private thought and feeling in every awakening sinner and in every saint? It is He,—it can only be He of whom it is said, "For the Spirit searcheth all things, yea, the deep things of God."

Personality and Deity of the Holy Spirit.

All the attributes of personality are manifest in Him. He is a Divine Person. We are baptized in His name; in his name we are blessed, as in the name of the Father and of the Son. The only sin which is unpardonable is committed against Him. He is not therefore "Divine influence." Christ would not need to go away that "Divine influence" might come. It is noticeable that the Bible never speaks as we do of "the influences of the Holy Spirit," but always refers to Him as a Person. "I will send Him unto you."

His Power Illustrated.

One illustration of the power with which the Holy Spirit works in human hearts, is seen in the rapid advancement of the first converts to Christianity. It is wonderful that the Epistles of the New Testament, which were to be the sufficient source of instruction for the Church of God in all times, should have been addressed to people so newly lifted out of heathenism. No such progress is made under the influence of letters as these converts from idolatry must have made, who were competent so soon to understand, for example, the Epistles to the Romans and to the Galatians. Such is the scale on which the Holy Spirit sets forward the human mind and heart. Creation only affords a parallel: "God who commanded the light to shine out of darkness hath shined in our hearts." We have all been struck with the sudden improvement in the minds, as well as characters, of people newly converted, — their good sense, their just perceptions. "The entrance of thy words giveth light; it giveth understanding unto the simple."

The infinite ease of the Holy Spirit's operation is full of encouragement. He does with one gentle thought, one secret, silent impression, that which reasoning and persuasion had utterly failed to accomplish. Often we expect a difficult work with a stubborn soul, but find it done. Laboring with great pains for a revival of religion in a Church and congregation, and meeting seemingly insuperable obstacles in the characters and conduct of many, — all at once you find your utmost hopes surpassed, and praise breaks forth "unto Him that is able to do exceeding abundantly above all that we ask or think, according to the power that worketh in us." We should begin every effort for the spiritual good of others with a calm sense of entire dependence upon the Holy Spirit, and of his almighty power, and saying, "So then neither is he that planteth, any thing, neither he that watereth." Thus we should pray and labor. Then we can continue; our efforts will be healthful; the excitement ministered by success will be the excitement of bracing air; and the joy of the Lord will be our strength. To the Holy Spirit belong all the appliances to be used in the conversion of the world.

The Holy Spirit is appointed to be the author of our whole spiritual experience. It is the Holy Spirit who makes the Saviour all that He is to us. What did we know of Christ till the Holy Spirit fulfilled that promise, "He shall receive of mine and shall show it unto you"?

Repentance and faith, with all the exercises of our renewed nature, are, from first to last, the work of the Holy Spirit. No more directly dependent are we on Christ for atoning blood than upon the Spirit for religious experience. Sanctification is from Him as peculiarly as justification is by Christ. And as "the Father judgeth no man, but hath committed all judgment unto the Son," so the Father and the Son have committed the entire work of "communion" to the Holy Spirit, this "communion" including even our fellowship with the Father and the Son; for as "no man knoweth who the Father is but the Son and he to whom the Son will reveal Him," so every act of love on our part toward God and Christ is by the Holy Spirit. Blessed Spirit! how little do we thank and love Thee! Beautiful, yea, how touching, is thy humility,— so willing to be subordinate, so little recognized by many of thine own! Like the parables, thy comparatively hidden nature may be intended to excite our faith, and draw us on to further knowledge. It is with Thee as it was with Him preceding Thee, who "came unto his own and his own received Him not." O Thou "seven Spirits which are before his throne!" Thou multiplicity, variety, and infinitude of spiritual powers and offices! it is only when we are spiritually-minded that we appreciate Thee! Silent, unseen, thy subordination also prevents us in a measure from thinking of Thee as we do of the Father and of the Son; and yet are we not baptized in thy name also? and in thy name we are blessed!

Nothing hinders us from believing that it was the third Person in the Godhead who is spoken of in Gen. i. 2: "And the Spirit of God moved upon the face of the waters." Incubating upon chaos, if then and there He deposited the seeds of things in the new elements, and created the original models of all forms in nature, organizing life in its endless manifestations, — it was in beautiful correspondence with his work, which is still greater, in the moral creation, as the author of regeneration, and of every thing which accompanies and flows from it. We see his work in the religious emotions experienced by the people of God, from the patriarch to the lisping child, from the first pang in conviction of sin, through the day-break of the new-born soul with its penitence, faith, and hope, — its conflicts, its victories, its discoveries, its spirit of adoption, its growing likeness to Christ. All this is his immediate work. Creator Spirit! to be "born of" Thee, to be "led by" Thee, to be "sanctified by" Thee, to have intercession made in us by Thee, and to be "sealed" by Thee to the day of redemption, — is worthy to be, as it is, the purchase and the gift even of the incarnation and the cross!

He made the Bible.

The Bible is the work of the Holy Spirit as distinctively as the cross pertains to Christ. It was proposed to make a book for the human race. Was there ever a more difficult undertaking? It is finished. Its plan, its details, none but infinite wisdom could arrange. Who should write it; what its contents should be; how much of history, and what histories; how much of legislation, of biography, prophecy, maxim, song; and in what ages, what countries, amid what manners and customs it should be composed; what length of time it should cover; and, no less difficult than all, what should be left out of it; in a word, how it should be, on the whole, best adapted to the use of all peoples and languages in every condition and stage of life,—all this was solved by Him to whom we owe the Bible. He devised the narrative of Joseph. He prepared the books of Esther and Ruth. He indited the Apocalypse. He taught Moses, inspired Daniel, inflamed Isaiah, breathed upon John. Sometimes we see a man doing a difficult work with an ingenious instrument devised and shaped by himself. The Holy Spirit made the Bible as the great instrument in his work. He made it for you, foreseeing your necessities; He helps you in reading it.

Descending from the contemplation of it as a

masterpiece of infinite wisdom, select one of its writers, and think what the communion of the Holy Ghost must have been with him,— for example, David. "Now these be the last words of David. David, the son of Jesse, said, and the man that was raised up on high, the anointed of the God of Jacob, and the sweet psalmist of Israel, said, 'The Spirit of God spake by me and his word was in my tongue.'" This was his most grateful recollection when reviewing life. In the progress of divine tuition, shall we not each of us, fellow-heirs of life! have received from the same Holy Spirit, who "dwelleth with" us "and shall be in" us, as much of communion, and as many great, ennobling, rapturous, and peace-inspiring thoughts as fell to the lot of David? One purpose of God in raising him up and endowing him, seems to have been to show us what He will hereafter do in spiritual things to all who love Him. "I will give you," says He, "the sure mercies of David."

THE INTERCESSION OF THE HOLY SPIRIT.

His connection with our private, spiritual life is brought to view when it is said, "Likewise the

Spirit also helpeth our infirmities; for we know not what we should pray for as we ought, but the Spirit itself maketh intercession for us with groanings which cannot be uttered. And He that searcheth the heart knoweth what is the mind of the Spirit, because He maketh intercession in the saints according to the will of God."

The meaning of this passage is not that the Holy Spirit intercedes in heaven for us. "For there is one God, and one mediator between God and men, the Man Christ Jesus." The Holy Spirit makes intercession "for us," by filling us with spiritual emotions so deep and strong that we cannot utter them except in "groanings." They are not unintelligible to God. He discerns their meaning more clearly than the laboring soul itself can either express or comprehend the object of the Holy Spirit when filling us with these earnest desires; and God regards these desires, because the Holy Spirit excites them. It seems, indeed, a singular way of helping our infirmities, to make us feel them all the more, and until we groan; yet this is the divine method, for, "when I am weak, then am I strong." *When our Christian feelings are such that words seem weak, the Holy Spirit is making intercession for us, by working in us.*

What encouragement there is in having the apostle Paul say, " We know not what we should pray for as we ought!" and in perceiving that he had the same spiritual "infirmities," and the same need of the Comforter, as we.

His Presence with a Church.

The chief desire and effort of every Christian Church should be to secure his constant presence. Every thing which tends to disturb harmony, and to make alienation and contention, is quenched by his indwelling in the hearts of Christians. Long-standing griefs and seemingly insuperable difficulties melt away at his coming. In honor "preferring one another," and bearing one another's burdens, there are no jealousies and envyings; mutual love prevails over every tendency to alienation. Weaknesses and faults in others cultivate the Christian graces of each. There is nothing, perhaps, in effect, so much like heaven as this. Our Congregational Church-organization offers peculiar opportunities for such experience; for the government not being vested in one man, or in a select body, the whole brotherhood have opportunities in their frequent intercourse to manifest those graces of the Spirit which Christian communion is fitted to develop. On the other hand, the liberty and equality conferred on all expose us to peculiar temptations; and, unless the Holy Spirit rules in our hearts, scenes may be enacted which will remind you that " there was war in heaven." But praying and laboring with one heart and one mind for the constant presence of the Holy Spirit, and being led by Him, the members of a Church become " a holy temple in the Lord;" to which others are brought, and are " builded together" with them " for an habitation of God through the Spirit."

The Ministration of the Spirit reaches through Time.

The work of redemption is to be finished by the Holy Spirit. Some ascribe the termination of efforts for the world's conversion to the interposition of Christ in person. We cannot properly enter here upon the consideration of this subject, but we may be sure that the third Person in the Godhead will not fail of his worthy share in the plan of salvation. The ministration of the Spirit is spoken of (2 Cor. iii.), in antithesis to the old dispensation, as though it would be the complement of the great redemptive work. Compared with the former dispensation it is to be "the rather glorious." The conception is sublime of this unseen Spirit carrying on, by his mysterious agency, and in perfect consistency with the free agency of men, good and bad, the stupendous work of subduing the world to Christ.

So He fulfils the Saviour's comparison of Him to the wind, which breathes on the softly-bending corn, or stirs the differing murmurs in the leaves of different trees, or comes as the trade-wind of commerce, or moves, at one and the same moment, all ships on every sea and ocean, from whatever quarter, and to whatever point they sail. Surely his name, also, shall be called "Wonderful." The very close of the Bible and of prophecy echoes his voice: "And the Spirit and the bride say, Come;" for the honor due to his name requires that his work in redemption continue to the end, and be commensurate with that of the Father and the Son.

He is "The Eternal Spirit."

The future relation of the Holy Spirit to the redeemed in heaven is a pleasing subject of contemplation. Never can your love to your Redeemer fail of vast accessions through the ages of your heavenly experience; it cannot be supplanted; on the contrary, the love which the Holy Spirit will receive from you will spring from sources which must enhance the love which you will feel toward the Father and the Son. But when we come to know, in full, the personal connection which the Holy Spirit had with us,—then Bethlehem, Gethsemane and Calvary will, perhaps, have their counterparts in places, seasons, and events of spiritual history, identified with the work of the Holy Spirit. "Now I beseech you, brethren, for the Lord Jesus Christ's sake and for the love of the Spirit," says Paul. Indeed, He must be a loving Spirit who does such acts of loving-kindness, so patiently, so gently, so tenderly, that the affection excited by our misdeeds and perverseness is not wrath but grief, because it is said, "And grieve not the Holy Spirit of God, whereby ye are sealed unto the day of redemption." Of course, the third Person in the Godhead does not merely accomplish an earthly mission for our souls; He will have a relation, no doubt, to our whole spiritual existence for ever. If conversion, if repentance, and faith, and the fruits of the Spirit, in our imperfect state be so wonderful, viewed as mental experiences, what must our experiences in heaven be, with the author of these present experiences still in some specific relation to us corresponding to his work here as Comforter! There we shall begin aright; all our mistakes and follies, prejudices and antipathies, will be removed; we shall have no bias to evil, no law in our members warring against the law of our mind. It will be the Holy Spirit Who will have set us right. Personal indebtedness to those who taught us useful knowledge here, who formed our opinions, led us into the path of discovery, and stimulated our powers, is a faint representation of our love and gratitude to Him who, we shall then see, was, in all the history of our minds and hearts, and in every sense of the word, — our " Comforter."

Every Christian has implanted in him now the

germ of each perfection which he will have in heaven. Hence the Holy Spirit is said to be "the earnest of our inheritance, the pledge of the purchased possession;" and, when we believed, we are said to have been "sealed with that Holy Spirit of promise,"—like the wine which receives the vintner's seal and is left to develop itself, only that there is in the soul a constant presence and agency of the Comforter. Regenerated persons, therefore, are "a chosen generation, a royal priesthood, a peculiar people." Poor, ignorant, lowly, though some of them may be, they are higher than the kings of the earth who are yet in their sins. Leading others to be of this "chosen generation" is the work in which we aid when we bring a soul to God. "For we are laborers together with God." Of such and of their labors, the Saviour said, "And he that reapeth receiveth wages, and gathereth fruit unto life eternal."

The World does not Know Him.

"Whom the world cannot receive, because it seeth Him not, neither knoweth Him." Infinite loss, never to know Him! "The natural man receiveth not the things of the Spirit of God, for they are foolishness unto him; neither can he know them, for they are spiritually discerned." Such were we. None can express or estimate the difference made in us by regeneration. This work of the Holy Spirit in us is likened to the creation of light; more than once it is ascribed to the same power which raised up Jesus from the dead. Have you had this new birth? Then God has done the greatest work in you which He ever accomplishes in the soul of man. What if God should visibly make an angel of some one whom we know and love! Let Him regenerate your soul, and hereafter you will have no occasion to covet an angel's nature, or his bliss. But in further contrast to the world's ignorance, the Holy Spirit imparts to ministers and Christians that indescribable gift called " unction." In preaching, in praying, in conversation, in spirit, in manner, in one's whole influence upon others, — this indefinable gift does more than genius, or talent, or learning, or zeal. It cannot be affected; the possessor is unconscious of it; the observer cannot tell what it is; but the Holy Spirit bestows it upon all in whom He specially loves to dwell. But the soul which never receives the Holy Ghost, will be in endless chaos. Disorder and darkness will possess it. For if we are born but once, we shall die twice; and if we are born twice, we shall die but once. "On such the second death hath no power."

Subordination of the Holy Spirit.

To the regenerate it may be useful to say, that subordination on the part of the Holy Spirit, so plainly declared, is a beautiful and powerful example of the same thing among Christians. Subordination in Christ is used by the apostle for the same purpose. "Let the same mind be in you which was also in Christ Jesus, who being in the form of God thought it not robbery to be equal with God, but made himself of no reputation, and took upon Him the form of a servant."

This was suggested by the exhortation, "Look not every man on his own things, but every man also on the things of others." With our Redeemer making himself of no reputation, but humbling himself; with our Sanctifier subordinating himself, surely we should ever be gentle and kind, seeking not our own, "but every man another's wealth."

UNCONDITIONAL PROMISE OF THE HOLY SPIRIT.

The Holy Spirit is the only gift which is unconditionally promised. We may pray for life or health or any other blessing, and it may not be consistent for God to grant our prayer. But such are the arrangements of Divine providence and grace, that sincere desires for the Holy Spirit can no more be disregarded than the desire of a child for food. To disregard our desires for the Holy Spirit is compared by Christ to the act of putting a stone into the hand of a child beseeching for bread; or imposing upon his ignorance by giving him, instead of a fish, a scorpion, which he would not know enough to distinguish from a fish. Such is the blessed Redeemer's assurance to every soul who reads these lines, that a true desire for the greatest and best gift which God can impart can never be preferred in vain.

Those words of Christ, "The wind bloweth where it listeth;—so is every one that is born of the Spirit," are not limited to conversion. Every one that is born of the Spirit will enjoy through life this mysterious agency of the Spirit. This should comfort and encourage those who are afraid, that, if they become Christians, they shall not persevere. Is not the atonement for your sins a divine work, and a full, complete provision for your justification? The Holy Spirit will complete his work, as surely as Christ has completed his. Only do with regard to Him as you have done in believing in Christ; that is, place your entire dependence, for continuance and progress, upon the Holy Spirit; and you "shall never fall." God will "go before thee, and be thy rearward."

What a stupendous plan of redemption this is, dear Christian friends, in which we believe! You are the subjects of that plan. It is worthy to be considered that the mode of the divine existence is disclosed to us only in connection with the development of redemption. The revelation, that Christ "was in the beginning with God and was God," seems to be made because a knowledge of the way of salvation rendered it necessary that this should appear. We learn the deity of the Holy Spirit chiefly in connection with his work in our souls. Let us consider what it is to be a member of the race whose history thus brings to view the mystery of the Godhead; and what it is to be one of that chosen number to whom alone this stupendous work is applied. Consider, too, that such a scheme of salvation, in which the Godhead is thus occupied, must have a counterpart of perdition corresponding to this salvation. What exaggeration, what superfluity of effort, what unnecessary endeavor, there would seem to be here, if all men can after all be saved by discipline!

To have been an object of this redemption, but to fail of being redeemed, and for ever to be sinking as low as, by redemption, you would have been exalted, will be intolerable,—more so, even, than the experience of those who fell from heaven and had no Redeemer.

If you who read these lines are not a partaker of the grace which the Holy Spirit imparts, you still may be. He has not withdrawn from you, for a subject like this would not attract and hold your attention, and awaken desire, were you given up to hardness of heart. Even you can be born again. With infinite ease, the Comforter can make you a new creature. Were there nothing supernatural in conversion, Christ would not have thrown such a mystery about a religious change as He does in his comparison of it to the wind. He calls it, also, being "born again." There is a divine, supernatural element, in conversion; and it is the best part of it. If God creates you anew, that new creation is as indestructible as the soul itself. Let me beg of you to pause just here,—wherever you are,—close your eyes, and address a prayer to the Holy Spirit, the Comforter. It is He who will have put it into your heart thus to pray; therefore, He is waiting to seal you to the day of redemption. Your views and feelings, your temper, disposition, frames of mind, tones of voice, in short, your whole consciousness, will be under his direction. He is so essential, that Christ left the world in order that the Holy Spirit might come. He has long striven with you, patiently, and with great forbearance. If the only sin which is unpardonable is a sin against Him, all sins against Him, it would seem, must have peculiar heinousness. For He is the ultimate remedy; the cross itself is in vain without Him. Let Him prevail with you. He will be to you all that Christ was to the disciples. He is " the earnest of heaven in our hearts."

The Man Christ Jesus owed every thing to Him. So will you,— present grace, and, in its largest sense, "communion" here; and, "He will show you things to come."

> Come, thou Holy Spirit! come,
> And, from thine eternal home,
>   Shed the ray of light divine:
> Come, thou Father of the poor,
> Come, thou Source of all our store,
>   Come, within our bosoms shine.
>
> Thou, of comforters the best;
> Thou, the soul's most welcome guest;
>   Sweet refreshment here below!
> In our labor, rest most sweet;
> Grateful shadow from the heat;
>   Solace in the midst of woe.
>
> O most blessed Light divine!
> Shine within these hearts of thine,
>   And our inmost being fill:
> If thou take thy grace away,
> Nothing pure in man will stay;
>   All our good is turned to ill.
>
> Heal our wounds, our strength renew,
> On our dryness pour thy dew,
>   Wash the stains of guilt away:
> Bend the stubborn heart and will,
> Melt the frozen, warm the chill,
>   Guide the steps that go astray.
>
> On the faithful who adore
> And confess thee, evermore,
>   In thy sevenfold gifts descend:
> Give them virtue's sure reward;
> Give them thy salvation, Lord;
>   Give them joys that never end.
>
>   Hymns Ancient and Modern.

Addresses to Church Members

BY THE

CONGREGATIONAL PASTORS OF BOSTON,

RECOMMENDED BY THE

Boston Congregational Council.

The following are now published, and ready for delivery: —

No. 1. THE RESULT OF COUNCIL. Complete.

No. 2. THE CHRISTIAN'S RECONSECRATION. By Rev. E. K. ALDEN, Pastor of Phillips Church.

No. 3. THE WORLDLINESS OF NOMINAL CHRISTIANS. By Rev. Dr. WEBB, Pastor of Shawmut Church.

No. 4. THE DUTY OF CHRISTIANS TO UNITE WITH SOME CHURCH, AND THE DUTY OF CHURCH-MEMBERS TO UNITE WITH THE CHURCH WHERE THEY STATEDLY WORSHIP. By Rev. S. P. FAY, Pastor of Salem Church.

No. 5. THE DUTY OF DAILY SECRET PRAYER and DAILY STUDY OF THE BIBLE. By Rev. J. M. MANNING.

No. 6. REVIVALS OF RELIGION. By Rev. J. E. TODD.

No. 7. THE DIVINE SOVEREIGNTY IN ITS RELATION TO HUMAN SALVATION. By Rev. Mr. BAKER.

No. 8. THE DUTY OF A MORE STRICT OBSERVANCE OF THE SABBATH. By Rev. Dr. BLAGDEN.

No. 9. THE POWER OF PRAYER. By Rev. Dr. KIRK.

No. 10. THE POWER AND OFFICE OF THE HOLY SPIRIT. By Rev. Dr. ADAMS.

The remaining Addresses will follow at intervals of about one week: viz: —

THE SPREAD OF THE GOSPEL IN THE CITY AMONG THE POOR, AND THOSE WHO HABITUALLY NEGLECT THE SERVICES OF THE SABBATH. By Rev. Dr. DEXTER.

THE CHRISTIAN'S DUTY TO WORK FOR THE SAVING OF SOULS. By Rev. Mr. BINGHAM.

No. 11. Published by direction of the Congregational Churches of Boston.

THE

DUTY OF CHRISTIANS

TO LABOR FOR THE

SALVATION OF SOULS.

BY

Rev. J. S. BINGHAM.

BOSTON:
NICHOLS AND NOYES.
1866.

THE

DUTY OF CHRISTIANS

TO LABOR FOR THE

SALVATION OF SOULS.

BY

Rev. J. S. BINGHAM.

.

BOSTON:
NICHOLS AND NOYES.
1866.

Entered according to Act of Congress, in the year 1860, by

NICHOLS AND NOYES,

In the Clerk's Office of the District Court of the District of Massachusetts.

CAMBRIDGE:
STEREOTYPED AND PRINTED BY JOHN WILSON AND SONS.

DUTY OF CHRISTIANS TO LABOR FOR THE SALVATION OF SOULS.

It will be taken for granted in the work now in hand, that souls still in the bondage of sin need to be saved. We shall assume, that, if Jesus came to seek and save the lost, there were lost to be sought and saved. We are not to attempt to prove the urgency of a work which has no existence. Souls which have not been renewed by the regenerating power of the grace of God are in a state of condemnation and death, and must be rescued; or that condition will prove an eternal one. We shall assume the importance of the work *on earth*, from the nature of the case, and the teachings of Christ. The only point now before us is, On whom is the responsibility devolved of laboring to secure the result? Here is a work to be done: who is to do it? Is the duty resting on a set-apart and ordained few, or on the redeemed and consecrated many? We believe every Christian to be under the highest obligations to labor for the rescue of those still unsaved. With these assumptions and qualifications, we may, perhaps, with profit, consider some reasons, *why it is the duty of Christians to labor for the salvation of souls.*

1. And we shall discover the first reason in the fact, that the Christian has struck the same law of action that actuates the Divine mind, which law is: *what can be wisely done for the salvation of souls ought to be done.*

So deep is the love of God, so pure is His compassion, and so determined His opposition to sin, that truthfulness to His own nature requires Him to do all He can wisely do to arrest its progress; and save those who have thrown themselves into its power, and subjected themselves to its fearful results. For "sin, when it is finished, bringeth forth death,"—death to manhood,—death to human affection,—death to sonship with God, and all its present and eternal rewards and privileges. It did not seem right to the Divine mind to allow the sinner to remain in this state of moral and spiritual ruin into which he had voluntarily plunged himself. Not that the law was unholy or unreasonable; not that the retributions for its breach were not ordained in infinite wisdom, love, and righteousness; but that, if any thing *could be done* in harmony with the eternal principles of Divine economy in moral and spiritual relations, it ought to be done. God could not be true to Himself, true to His own ideas of redemption,— which ideas are as fundamental as those of the creation of moral beings,— and leave the sinner to perish without His intervention, *His working to save him.* Hence Jesus "was slain from the foundation of the world." This could be done. The law could not be changed; its retributions could not be annulled, for these were in their nature immutable; but Jesus could come and receive the consequences of the sinner's guilt upon His own heart, and send back a current of life from that heart to regenerate and redeem the sinner. This He could do, and not move a single line in the infinite survey of Divine economy. And because He *could* do it, He was impelled by the law of *dutifulness to Himself* to say, "Lo! I come." Hence He says, "*Ought* not Christ to have suffered these things, and to enter into His glory?" as much as to say, It was needful for Christ to endure what He has for the sinner, in order to unfold the true glory of the Divine nature, and satisfy its yearning love.

But the Christian, by virtue of his regeneration and consecration, has received the same spirit, and become permeated with the same ideas and principles. The same mind which was in Christ is in him. The same law of action, the same law of sacrifice, moves him. If Jesus felt that truthfulness to the Divine nature in Him required Him to do what He has done to save the sinner; if, in this sense, He felt He *must* do what *could*— and, therefore, *ought* to—be done, the same spirit and principle will actuate and energize the Christian,— every Christian. If Christ came to seek and to save the lost, because He was constrained by the yearning of His own eternal love, the same love must and will constrain His disciple.

Here then is the foundation of Christian

duty in this regard. It rests on this principle: it is not right, is not consistent with the nature and character of "our Father" to permit the sinner to live and perish in his sins without doing all that can be wisely done for his redemption. We say *wisely*, because it is manifest that what cannot be wisely done, in moral relations, cannot be done at all. This is the ground of God's action. It must be the ground of duty for the Christian. He cannot be true to God; true to his own nature, — now renewed, and sanctified; true to the needs of his fellow-men, without going to the extreme boundary of his capacity in laboring for the salvation of souls. This, if we mistake not, is the highest idea of *duty*. It fuses sympathy and love with unchangeable righteousness. It declares, it is not right to permit our neighbor to commit moral suicide. It is not right to allow our children to perish in the flames, although they are very wicked children; and have disobeyed our kind, but positive, instructions, and set the house on fire over their heads. It demands of us to rush into the flames, and pluck men as brands from the burning. It charges us to hedge up the ruinous way of the sinner with every possible means of grace, with Bibles and sermons, with expostulations and arguments, with entreaties and prayers, with floods of tears, and the gushing blood of agony, if so be he may be arrested in his mad career of death, and turned back into the way of holiness and life. It bids us plead, "Father, forgive them: they know not what they do." It bids us stand between the living and the dead, and stay the sweeping malady. If men are so far gone as to be utterly indifferent to the claims of God, and completely reckless in regard to their own eternal interests, we must be all the more in earnest. Out into the highways and hedges of the country, the streets and lanes of the city, must we urge our way; and compel the most thoughtless to think, the most hardened to feel, and the most stubborn to yield. As God did not wait for perishing sinners to apply for His redemption in saving grace, so Christians must not wait for awakened sinners to ask to be guided to the fountain of salvation. We must go, unasked; we must persevere, although resisted. We have thrown ourselves into the current of infinite love, demanding, as a *duty*, the utmost that can be done to save the sinner. And this principle presses upon, and springs up within, every Christian, without exception. It conquers all reluctance and timidity, all reserve and natural frigidness. It bursts forth, like a blazing Hecla, amid gathering icebergs and snow-capped mountains. So deep and mighty is the vital force, so perfectly is the life united to, and " hidden with, Christ in God," that it must have utterance. It is a law of duty springing from the heart, as well as the wisdom, of God; inspiring every heart which has ever felt the regenerating power of saving grace.

2 But we may see another reason for this in the fact, *that Christians are now the body of Christ on earth.*

While Jesus our Lord was here in person, " He possessed a body in which he went about doing good." In this, He manifested God in the flesh. In this, He glorified, unfolded, brought out to view, the nature and thoughts of God. In this, He developed the power of Divinity working through the agency of humanity,— a Divine soul revealing itself as united with, and exercising complete control over, a human soul and body. But that soul, and that body spiritualized, Christ has taken with Him to heaven. In the place of this humanity, in the place of this human soul and body, He has placed His believers. Every Christian is now the humanity, the body, the objectiveness, the manifestation of Christ in the flesh, in the place where in the providence of God he may be located. Christians are now His willing feet, His outstretched hands, His persuasive lips, His tremulous voice, His weeping eyes. His yearning, redeeming, agonizing love is now to be manifested through the life and preaching and prayers of His disciples. His Spirit uses Philip as His earthly humanity to guide the inquiring eunuch to the Saviour he sought; He uses Peter as His body at Jerusalem and Cesarea; Paul, at Damascus, Ephesus, Athens, and Rome; and His disciples, everywhere "scattered abroad," "preaching the word." His Spirit enters into His disciples, and inspires them as preachers, writers, publishers, teachers, and laborers in every department of work for the relief of human woe, and the salvation of ruined souls. In His name, in His power, and in His stead, they go forth; and, if they abide in Him, whatsoever they shall ask shall be done for them. If His Spirit strives within them in "groanings which cannot be uttered," how speedily will He answer them!

If then Christians are faithful, and really *consecrated* to their work, — *His work*, — Christ will have as many souls and bodies, through which to seek the lost, as there are believers in Him. This has been adopted as the best and closing dispensation in God's kingdom on earth. It has seemed best thus to blend Divinity with human thought, sympathy, love, and faith, in the work of saving souls. It was expedient for Christ in person to go away in order that the Holy Ghost, whom He would send in his name, might be conferred upon the whole Church; and the gospel be more universally preached to every creature. For as, in the physical world God can most wisely erect temples, construct ships, and build railroads through the agency of the skill and workmanship of man, while He carves out the continents and lifts up the mountains without such agency; so can He, in the spiritual world, best redeem and save sinners through the co-operation of those already rescued. Having chosen this plan as the best, — as His choosing it proves, — the duty is imperative upon every one who has been reached and quickened by the power of God, most earnestly and faithfully to manifest His love in every appointed way. If Christians are true temples of the Holy Ghost; if He abides with them continually, and is ever struggling in their souls to be uttered; if He strives to make the humanity in which He lives speak His words, obey His guidance, and breathe His petitions; if God is stretching out His hands of compassion to the perishing through those who have covenanted with Him, as much as in them lies, to represent and make effectual His unceasing love and pardoning grace, — can there be any question respecting duty? If Christians are to be so many editions of the life of Christ; so many living commentaries on His teachings; so many illustrations of the meaning of "regeneration, sanctification, and redemption;" so many wills, repeating all along the whole line of humanity, the commands, the warnings, and the invitations of God, — is there still any ground for debate concerning duty? There is no avoiding the obligation save in renouncing allegiance to God, separating ourselves from Christ, and refusing to be the temples of the Holy Ghost. If we are not laboring for the salvation of souls, we are not the body of Christ, and we do not bear the fruit of His heart. We are only nominal branches; and must, sooner or later, be removed.

3. *We shall discover another reason for this duty in the peculiar efficiency of its earnest discharge.*

If God has made any thing clear in these days, it is the amazing power of the people. The idea of the Divine right of a few to govern the many is exploded. The governing and redeeming power of the people is most signally owned of God as His own appointment. When He has secured in the hearts of the people "a mind to work," His great designs of human salvation and elevation are rapidly achieved. When this marvellous latent energy can be aroused, quickened, and brought out into wise and earnest work, the most glorious results are witnessed. We see this in times of revival. Christians *as a body* are then at work,— as they ought to be all the time, — "every one over against his own house," and in his place of business, with his neighbors, in the "people's meeting" for conference and prayer. The masses of impenitent persons are moved because the Spirit of God in the masses of Christians has utterance. Many souls are saved because many are working and praying to that end. It is not the minister and a few "leading members" only who are now at work manifesting the love of Christ, but the democratic element of power is now in active operation. The constitution of the human heart is the same as before; the truth is the same; God is the same; His readiness to hear and answer prayer, and reward labor, is only the same: but the people are changed. They are now *personally* laboring directly to save souls; and so long as they continue in that work will the revival continue, whether it be for weeks, months, or years. There will be greater *manifestations* of the Spirit's presence at some times than at others, but the real work will go on continually. It is the perpetual, personal labor of every Christian which occasions the leaven rapidly to leaven the whole lump. The leavened works on that portion of the unleavened with which it comes in contact. Christians are scattered through the whole community, in which the gospel has attained a good measure of success; and the Spirit of God has thus a humanity, through which to work in every department of society.

Sinners will cavil over the Bible, give away preaching, and question the printed page; but the consistent, earnest, warm-hearted Christian, who personally cares for their souls, gains access to the heart, and leads them into the kingdom of God. Bibles and well-selected libraries are priceless treasures on shipboard, but a skilful, resolute, courageous, Christian sailor, who lives and talks the Bible, and converses with his shipmates concerning the eternal interests of their souls, will accomplish more than they all. What then shall we say concerning his *duty?* What shall we say of the duty of every Christian who has any mode of personal access to men? What shall we say of the duty of Christians scattered abroad, and daily coming in contact with those who never visit the sanctuary, or come within the reach of any other means of grace? The press and the pulpit can do much, but the working people can do immeasurably more. They can make every house and work-shop, every market-place and highway, a place of "speaking for Jesus." Instead of leaving their avocations because they are converted, they make the fact, that men must meet them on business in these avocations, an occasion for doing something for the salvation of their souls. Men are shy of those who make it their profession to save souls, but feel at home with their daily associates; and a few words from these will often have more power over them than the most elaborate sermons.

And men are never too much in a hurry to speak or hear a word in this direction, if that is made the engrossing topic. When we were struggling to save the nation, we were never too much in haste to say, "Good news to-day;" "Glorious victory, that!" "God is helping us." So when Christians make the salvation of souls the great business of life, and all transactions in the things needful for the body only its incidentals, they always will find time to say, "Come to Jesus;" "I hope you love the Saviour." If Christians will surrender themselves to be used

THE DUTY OF CHRISTIANS. 17

by the Spirit of God, and permit Christ to speak through them at all times and in all places, we shall see the kingdom of God coming with power and glory. If every individual Christian will reduce this, his chief business, to system, throwing his inventive power into it to discover the best means he can use; if he will throw his entire human force, sanctified and permeated by the Divine, into this work, the will of God will soon be done on earth as in heaven. Should every Christian, like a man of business, carry his pocket-memorandum with its list of " persons to be seen ; " " individuals to be conversed with to-day; " " subjects for this week's prayers ; " " cases of conversion ascertained ; " " urgent, present demands ; " "*persons not to be unduly urged ;* " there can be no estimate of the results. There can be no more question of success in this matter than in any other in which men rightly and earnestly engage. God has determined to bless persevering work ; He always has crowned it; He will — He does, *now*. It is in harmony with His own action, and the laws of the human mind. It imparts life and vigor to the laborer. It intensifies his consecration, and hastens his sanctification. It gives directness in effort, and peculiar power and prevalence in prayer. He has an object in his will, a burden upon his heart, and a glorious result in his faith. He has struck the idea of Jesus, when He pleads, "I pray not that Thou shouldst take them out of the world." There is work to be done; souls to be saved; Divine love to be carried to the perishing; Christ's work on earth to be perpetuated, and advanced to complete triumph through human forces. With every Christian thus laboring, praying, and trusting in God, there is no more doubt, that every Christian Church in the world can double its numbers each successive year, than there can be doubt in the promises and faithfulness of God. This is bringing in "all the tithes," this is doing all we know how to do; and the windows of heaven will surely be opened over us, and a blessing poured out which there shall not be room to receive. Is there then any question of duty? We, *the people*, possess the most effective power through which the Holy Spirit can bring the truth to bear upon the heart of unregenerate men. We possess human sympathy, and human experience,—the experience of being once lost, but now found; once wrecked, but now rescued; once "starving prisoners," but now at home, amid its peace and plenty and unspeakable joy. And shall we forget the lost, still wandering; the wrecked, still tossing amid the breakers; the prisoners, still starving? Shall we smother all this force, and "quench the Spirit" who would use it to save souls? Oh! it is time to act. It is time to "do with our might." It is time to do, *because we can.* It is time to avoid the curse of *not doing.* We cannot always live *on being forgiven.* We must some time find our meat in doing the will of our Father in heaven. Shall we begin now? Let us do it, and we shall soon receive the Saviour's forgiving "Come, ye blessed," and His approving "Well done."

Addresses to Church Members

BY THE

CONGREGATIONAL PASTORS OF BOSTON,

RECOMMENDED BY THE

Boston Congregational Council.

The following are now published, and ready for delivery: —

No. 1. THE RESULT OF COUNCIL. Complete.

No. 2. THE CHRISTIAN'S RECONSECRATION. By Rev. E. K. ALDEN, Pastor of Phillips Church.

No. 3. THE WORLDLINESS OF NOMINAL CHRISTIANS. By Rev. Dr. WEBB, Pastor of Shawmut Church.

No. 4. THE DUTY OF CHRISTIANS TO UNITE WITH SOME CHURCH, AND THE DUTY OF CHURCH-MEMBERS TO UNITE WITH THE CHURCH WHERE THEY STATEDLY WORSHIP. By Rev. S. P. FAY, Pastor of Salem Church.

No. 5. THE DUTY OF DAILY SECRET PRAYER and DAILY STUDY OF THE BIBLE. By Rev. J. M. MANNING.

No. 6. REVIVALS OF RELIGION. By Rev. J. E. TODD.

No. 7. THE DIVINE SOVEREIGNTY IN ITS RELATION TO HUMAN SALVATION. By Rev. Mr. BAKER.

No. 8. THE DUTY OF A MORE STRICT OBSERVANCE OF THE SABBATH. By Rev. Dr. BLAGDEN.

No. 9. THE POWER OF PRAYER. By Rev. Dr. KIRK.

No. 10. THE POWER AND OFFICE OF THE HOLY SPIRIT. By Rev. Dr. ADAMS.

No. 11. THE CHRISTIAN'S DUTY TO WORK FOR THE SAVING OF SOULS. By Rev. Mr. BINGHAM.

The last Number, completing the Series, will be published next week; viz: —

THE SPREAD OF THE GOSPEL IN THE CITY AMONG THE POOR, AND THOSE WHO HABITUALLY NEGLECT THE SERVICES OF THE SABBATH. By Rev. Dr. DEXTER.

No. 12.   Published by direction of the Congregational Churches of Boston.

THE

SPREAD OF THE GOSPEL

IN THE CITY,

AMONG THE POOR WHO HABITUALLY NEGLECT THE SANCTUARY.

BY

Rev. H. M. DEXTER, D.D.

BOSTON:
NICHOLS AND NOYES.
1866.

THE

SPREAD OF THE GOSPEL

IN THE CITY,

AMONG THE POOR WHO HABITUALLY
NEGLECT THE SANCTUARY.

BY

Rev. H. M. DEXTER, D.D.

BOSTON:
NICHOLS AND NOYES.
1866.

Entered according to Act of Congress, in the year 1866, by

NICHOLS AND NOYES,

In the Clerk's Office of the District Court of the District of Massachusetts.

CAMBRIDGE:
STEREOTYPED AND PRINTED BY JOHN WILSON AND SONS.

HOW SHALL THE GOSPEL BE SPREAD ABROAD IN THE CITY AMONG THE POOR WHO HABITUALLY NEGLECT THE SERVICES OF THE SANCTUARY?

THE following propositions may safely be assumed as the foundation of all just answer to this question; viz. : —

1st, Every man needs the Gospel; needs it for the well-being of this life scarcely less than for that of the life to come.

2d, Of all men, those who are contemplated in this question need the Gospel most,— if any such comparative estimate might be tolerated.

3d, The Gospel was Divinely shaped, and has been put in operation on the earth, for every man; with special fitnesses for the needy and neglected.

4th, God desires that every man should have it; and designs, when His purposes have taken time enough to ultimate themselves consistently with human free agency, that every man shall have it.

5th, His plan, for spreading it abroad, is to use human instrumentality; animated, guided, guarded, and supplemented by the Divine Spirit.

6th, That plan centres in the working of His Church; which, in one aspect, it would be right to name a human society, Divinely organized and endowed for the conversion of the world.

7th, Influence passes by contact; therefore the Gospel influence, which is in the Church for the salvation of the needy and the neglected, must be put into contact with them before it can bless them.

8th, As, by the supposition of the question, they will not come to the Gospel, the Gospel must go to them; and, since it cannot go except men carry it, it must be carried to them; and, since God has instituted the Church for just that service, it must be carried by the Church.

The real inquiry then before us is simply this: How shall the Churches of Christ, in this community, carry the Gospel effectively to the poor, who, by their habitual neglect of the Sabbath and the sanctuary, demonstrate at once the greatness of their need, and the difficulty of its supply?

I. It will be obviously safe to answer, negatively, that the work cannot be done without some action reaching out further than, and differing from, what are ordinarily called the "means of grace." Every Church may have its round of customary Sabbath and week-day services faithfully performed, while yet, almost within the daily sweep of the shadow of the spire of its meeting-house, men and women and children may be living and dying in a practical heathenism; as effectual, if not as obvious, as that of India or Japan. And this may be equally true, whether that meeting-house be habitually thronged, because of the magnetism of sanctified eloquence in its pulpit; or the reverse. The effect of the "means of grace" is upon those who are reached by them. Sabbath worship and prayer meetings are essential to instruct and edify and save those who attend upon them, and to fit them and prompt them to undertake to evangelize the masses; but *they* will not evangelize the masses.

II. Nor will the work be done by deputation,— the Churches associating to establish and endow some society to undertake what they vaguely feel to be their work, which they are conscious of failing to perform by their ordinary processes, and to which those processes seem inadequate, and indeed unfitted. Something can be done thus: something ought to be done thus. Our own City Missionary Society, with its twenty-one missionaries, sustained during the past year at an average cost of some thirteen hundred dollars to each of the ten contributing Churches, has accomplished, and is accomplishing, a good that would apparently be unmixed, if the very fact that it seems to too many of, and in, the Churches to be doing their duty in this thing for them, — to the degree of making them easy, as if all were doing which Christ expects, — were not a counterpoising evil which it is easier to observe than to estimate. Where many Churches share one field, and consequently divide its responsibility, there are some things of a spiritual nature, and more of the nature of that temporal relief which must always accompany (when it does not go before) the endeavor to carry the Gospel to the destitute, which can best be done by organized, associate labor. So that it is in all respects probable, that every wisely planned eleemosynary institution which now has existence, possibly with a very few additions to their number, will be needed and be pushed, with a constant increase of energy and efficiency, on to, and into, the millenium. But as these societies have not yet evangelized the masses,—indeed, with all the blessing that has been in them, have accomplished very little in that direction,—it does not need long reflection to settle it, that, from the nature of the case, much as they are needed in the absence of some better agency, they alone cannot do it. The work is too mighty for them, on the one hand; while they lack elements essential to success in doing it, on the other. The one hundred thousand farmers of Illinois might better depute the tillage of their acres to a society that should employ a few hundred of the best available agricultural laborers: because many of them have land that, by the stroke of a hoe, will burden itself with a harvest from one generation to another by its own richness, without the addition of an ounce of compost; while these moral fields are waste places, very Saharas of sterility, if indeed they are not jungles matted with thistles, and all manner of noxious and inveterate weeds. Twenty-one city missionaries—what are they among so many! Those now laboring in Boston are faithful and industrious and devoted men and women, as all who know them and their work will testify, but the best they could do last year was to reach with their salutary efficiency some nine thousand different families, — a fact, the mere mention of which, when one recalls the character of our great and fast enlarging population, is demonstration that the effect of their toil, beneficent as it is, can scarcely be expected to do more than check the downward drift of a great city, leaving us each year, perhaps, to thank God that as a community we are no worse than we were the year before; but failing utterly to grapple successfully with the problem of bringing the multitudes to the cross. The Rebellion never could have been crushed on the theory that the regiments composing our grand armies were at liberty to club together, and delegate the hard work of their campaigns to a selected few, in the proportion, say of twenty-one to every five thousand, — which is about that between the Boston city-missionaries and the Church-members who support them. And the Gospel never can include the masses of our population among its conquests, until we see and feel that such a course is as absurd in the tactics of grace as it would have been in those of patriotism.

And even if any such delegated labor could be made broad enough to cover the ground, it would still lack some of the best elements of fitness for the needful work. It is official, and so presents itself always at a disadvantage at the poor man's door. A neighbor, who drops in of an evening, evidently out of the kind impulse of a pious heart, will necessarily gain a readier access to his sympathies and his convictions than the best person whom he understands to be salaried for that purpose, and who comes because it is "so nominated in the bond." Such functional visitation will also be too infrequent for success, where, pre-eminently, "precept must be upon precept, precept upon precept; line upon line, line upon line; here a little, and there a little." And, chiefly, it fails to conform itself to the Divine plan; which, we might be sure from inference, as we must be sure from observation of the facts, was exactly fitted to the necessities of the human nature for whose redemption it was shaped, because Christ proposed and enjoined upon His redeemed ones a *personal* ministration of the Gospel to every creature in all the world; not an official one, by which certain individuals, either for themselves as individuals, or as the delegates or servants of the body, should undertake it. So far as what we technically know as "preaching the Gospel" is concerned,—which is a service of instruction and influence lying behind, prompting, and shaping all Church agencies,—it is appointed to a selected few. But so far as telling the good news of the cross to all men, and striving "by all means" to make all men disciples of Christ, is concerned,—which is precisely the duty which our Lord, in His last command, laid upon His friends and servants,—it is, in no sense, more the heritage or the privilege or the obligation of one disciple than of another; of the pastor, whose part in doing it may be chiefly to stand in the pulpit, than of the people, whose share permits them on the Sabbath-day to sit in pews and hear the Word. Christ has so arranged it, on the one hand, that the spiritual health and growth of every Christian shall require that daily exercise which will be furnished best by some benevolent contact with the needy and the neglected, in the endeavor to do them good; and, on the other, that such needy and neglected ones shall take Christian influence in a more kindly and effectual manner from such personal contact with individual, private Christians than in any other way. And so, by fitting the demand to the supply, and the supply to the demand, the great Head of the Church has made it clear that the chemistry of grace works best, as does the chemistry of nature, by a diffusive, molecular force, operating as it were through a succession of single combats, in which each atom of salt gets the better of each atom tending to decay; by which each atom of leaven lifts each atom of meal until the whole be sweetened and leavened.

This Divine plan, then, while it welcomes any and all wise expedients to assist in the great labor, — and that, more especially, so long as it remains unable to bring up its array of individual forces intelligently and efficiently to the work, — most clearly relies for victory upon the Churches themselves in all their membership, and not upon any workers selected from, or delegated by, them.

III. But, if the work of carrying the Gospel to

the poor who neglect the sanctuary is to be done by the Churches, yet is not to be accomplished by them without some putting forth of force and influence over, and outside of, the ordinary Church processes of the Sabbath and of the week, while that force and influence cannot be in any satisfactory measure made to do their work through deputation to the hands of the City Missionary, or any other society or organization or force whatsoever, it follows that the Churches must evangelize the masses by working in their own proper capacity as Churches upon them; yet, by the use of some system of Church agency, differing from, and going beyond, any thing ordinarily supposed to be included in the "means of grace." The following principles suggest all which needs to be said by way of indicating what this agency should be, in itself and in its processes of development.

1. Every Church should feel that the condition of the poor in this city who neglect the sanctuary and profane the Sabbath is a standing rebuke to every one of its members, and a perpetual reproach to its fair fame; that the Gospel, faithfully applied, may reasonably expect God's seconding to the extent of removing that re-

proach; that it is its duty to apply it, trusting in God for success; and therefore that nothing can excuse its neglect to undertake such faithful application.

2. Every Church should feel that this duty of thoroughly Christianizing the community, while in some respects and for some purposes resting upon the Church as a body, in other respects, and for the main purpose of WORK, rests upon *every member*. It should feel, that, while a member who is " apt to teach" may most usefully discharge, perhaps, the main part of his portion of personal responsibility by teaching, and one that can exhort well may perform a portion of his share of labor by exhortation, and one who can give may do a good deal of his part — never the whole — by giving, God and Christ release nobody; and that, in every way, " unto whomsoever much [of any and all kinds of gift, force, and influence] is given, of him shall be much required." It should feel therefore, that, with a scale exactly just, graduated in remembrance of gifts differing according to the grace that is given, " the great Head of the Church expects every Christian to do his duty, and relies, without exception, upon ALL as workers together with Him."

3. Every Church should feel that this work of evangelizing the masses, whatever else it may be, and whatever else may need to be done in the Church or out of it to secure success to its one great aim, must be, pre-eminently, one of direct personal contact between the Gospel in its possessors, and the sin and wretchedness to be removed. And this contact — since, as was said before, the classes needing especially to be reached will not come to the Gospel — must necessarily be effected by the Church-members, travelling out of their Church-home and surroundings to the abiding places of the need and vice which they would relieve and transform. Nothing short of this will secure that contact between the balm in Gilead and the Physician there, and the wretched and the lost, by which alone their spiritual health may be recovered. EVERY CHRISTIAN, A HOME MISSIONARY — is then the brief formula out of which evolves itself the true answer to the question before us.

In carrying out the general work indicated by these three principles, the following suggestions may be helpful: —

(1.) Let every Church accept this duty, — not blindly nor impulsively, but with a deliberate conception of, and assent to, the care, the toil, the self-denial which must of necessity be involved in it; expecting to be always repelled by much of the distasteful work which must be done, to be often discouraged, and sometimes well-nigh disheartened; ye determined to lay aside every weight, and r with patience the race that is set before it, looking unto Jesus, the author and finisher of faith, who, for the joy that was set before Him, endured the cross, despising the shame; and willing for His sake to crucify the flesh, with the affections as well as the lusts.

(2.) Let every Church use its utmost exertions, by wise instructions of the pulpit, and by frequent, specific endeavors in the prayer and conference meetings, so to quicken the Christian vitality of every one of its members, that each shall feel impelled to ask, "What wilt Thou have *me* to do?" and to say when workers are called for, "Here am I, send *me*." Let young converts be indoctrinated with that benign, missionary idea, that a sweet consciousness of humble, faithful work, done for Christ, and not an ecstatic feeling in the heart, is the truest and usefullest Christian experience. Let suitable words apprise every candidate for Church membership, that a new working bee, and not another drone, is the expectation of the hive concerning him. Let the Church officers having supervision of the outgoing labors of the Church take great pains to assign work wisely to the special aptitudes of each believer, so as to make that work as much a congenial employment of natural capacity as possible; seeking thus to lighten every one's share by making the yoke fit his neck, while at the same time thus largely augmenting the general amount of production. And let not the fact, that never in this imperfect world will any Church be able to bring all its members up to the point of seeing and accepting and discharging their individual responsibility to work for Christ, discourage or delay its making assault, with all whom it can muster, upon the kingdom of Satan. No regiment fought through the Rebellion, but they had an " awkward squad " and some deserters.

(3.) Let every Church not only accept the duty of carrying the Gospel to the needy and the neglected, but let it most firmly believe, that that work can be done, and that success is sure. Let it feed itself on the strong meat of prophecy until its eye of faith can see " houses of joy in the joyous city;" and the desert of pauperism blossoming as the rose, yea, blossoming abundantly, and rejoicing with joy and singing; and the ransomed of the Lord walking with songs and gladness where now lurk the ravenous beasts of lust and riot, and where the dragons of crime have their habitation. Let it inscribe in letters of cheering light upon the walls of its Church-house, " He *shall* see of the travail of his soul, and *shall be* satisfied." Let them meditate upon the almightiness of God and of His grace; and consider what a price has been paid for human redemption, and how much is at stake in this conflict between the devil and that Blessed One who " took part of the same, that through death He might destroy him" and deliver men; and let them eagerly note how, along all the ages of the Christian history, the providence of God has seemed always to lie in friendly wait for examples of individual and associate fidelity in order to lavish upon them the tokens of His loving appreciation, and make them exultingly know that He is able to do " exceeding abundantly above all that we ask or think," until they feel that triumph is certain; that, in

God, they too are almighty; that it is His good pleasure to give them the kingdom; and until every one of them can say, "I know both how to be abased, and I know how to abound, and to suffer need; and I can do all things through Christ, Which strengtheneth me."

. (4.) Accepting thus the duty, with all the available strength of its individual membership, and in that confidence in ultimate success which is warranted by the purposes, the promises, and providence of God, it would next be wise for the Church to have conference with its sister evangelical Churches for the purpose of deciding what exact portion of the common, outlying field properly lies within its Christian oversight. Between them, those Churches must necessarily be responsible to God for every family and every soul; remotely, to the extent of general agencies, if the disproportion between their strength and the broadness of the field forbids more; directly, with all particular labor, if a fair division of the territory reduces the neglected population, for which each Church is accountable, within a space which it may reasonably undertake to cover with all suitable ministrations of Christian activity and influence. Only by some equitable and exact division can it be made certain, on the one hand, that the labors of different Churches shall not overlap and interfere; and, on the other, that no portion of territory shall be overlooked and neglected by all.

It may probably be assumed, that an equitable division of the area of the city of Boston occupied by the class to which our question refers, between its evangelical Churches, in spaces proportioned to the membership of each, would give to each Church a territorial parish — not always adjacent to its house of worship — which it would be entirely reasonable for every such Church to accept as a field which, with the proper interest and effort of its membership, it might hope to cultivate for Christ with every reason to expect success.

(5.) The next step might wisely be to divide the territory thus assigned to, and accepted by, the Church into a great number of smaller portions, for assignment among the workers of the body. Of right, there should be as many of these subdivisions as there are Church-members, that each home missionary may have his field. But, probably, a subdivision into two or three hundred districts would be as far as it might be wise to go in this direction in any Church. On the one hand, that number would probably bring the size of the area assigned to each laborer down to from five to ten families (not as many if they are *very* hard cases), which are enough to tax the time, strength, sympathy, and means of the visitor; while, on the other, even in a Church of six or eight hundred active, present members, there will be so many who will be prevented by age or infirmity, or an over-pressure of home duty, or by some other good reason, — to say nothing of shirks and deserters, — from such service, that there will always be labor required to keep that number of sub-divisions manned up to their full working-power. It may be better to leave a part of the field temporarily unworked than to make these sub-districts too large. A very few families, who, living near together, can be called on, and kept the run of, in an hour or two, will be apt to be seen frequently enough to answer the best purpose, — as often perhaps as every week, certainly every fortnight. While a number so large as to involve great weariness, and so much time in going the rounds that the best that can be done is a hurried glance, and a tract thrown in at the door, and even that, perhaps, scarcely on the average once in a month, involves constant discouragement and final failure; for the same reason that a farmer's crop will be a failure if he have so much ground to go over that he does not see any one field between seed time and harvest time. It will be all work, and no harvest. And precisely this has been the miscalculation which has discouraged some Churches who have made a fair beginning, and run well for a time, in this species of effort.

(6.) Having thus prepared the way, the next step will be to secure the wise, kind, patient, prayerful working of these sub-divisions by the individual members of the Church. It should be the distinct understanding, on all hands, that to take the care of one of these districts — assigned with a wisdom which tenderly marks and meets the peculiar powers, fitnesses, and weaknesses, of each laborer — is the normal expectation which the Church has in regard to each of its members, unless good cause of release can be made out; is presumptively as much the duty of every one who enters into covenant with Christ and with his followers as it is to pray, to keep the Sabbath, and to grow in grace; as much his duty as it is the duty of the enlisted soldier to fight the battles of the nation. If the soldier be maimed or sick, or detailed for guard duty or for some clerkly service, he is thereby, for the time being, excused from the field; and if the Church-member be sick or maimed, or detailed for some engrossing home-duty, or for some collateral good work which throws the barrier of an impossibility between him and this labor, he may be excused from it; but in no other event. His unwillingness — indolent or otherwise — cannot excuse him from it; his distaste for it cannot excuse him from it, for "even Christ pleased not Himself," and "it is enough for the disciple that he be as his master, and the servant as his lord." God bids him do it: "For the poor shall never cease out of the land; therefore I command thee, saying, thou shalt open thine hand wide unto thy brother, to thy poor, and to thy needy, in thy land;" and He has declared that, before Him, the visiting of the fatherless and widows in their affliction shares the genuine essence of pure religion and undefiled, with keeping one's self unspotted from the world. Christ expects it of him, for He was anointed to preach the Gospel to the poor, to heal the broken-hearted, to save the children of the needy, to redeem their soul from deceit and violence, and to break in pieces the oppressor; and He says to us, "If any man serve Me, let him follow Me. . . . If ye love Me, keep My commandments." He describes the purpose which he has in calling us into His Church, and so maintaining its existence on the earth, by saying, "Ye are the light of the world." And, when it is dark, men do not light a candle and shut it up under a bushel; but they lift it up on a candlestick, that it may give light unto all in the house: and so we are driven to the inference that these Churches of Christ in Boston are not well managed, not grateful in His sight, when their light is concentrated and secluded in their meetinghouses and rooms for prayer, so that just only a few feeble rays may stream out through the windows, and the cracks of the doors, to illumine surrounding darkness; but their light ought to be carried outside, so that the darkest corners may be cheered and helped by it. When children are lost, lantern-bearers are wanted as well as street lights; and the poor who habitually neglect the Sabbath and the sanctuary are pre-eminently "the lost" whom Christ came to seek and to save, and the seeking and saving of whom, He has bequeathed as His legacy of service to them — and to all of them, without exception — that love and would follow Him in every age.

Unless, then, a man or a woman professing Christianity is prepared to prove facts which make his or her case a clear singularity, lying outside of all the general rules of grace, he or she must necessarily admit the duty of sharing with others those habitual toils of Christian charity which may be both most wisely and easily administered by falling into the system of sub-division which has been advocated and explained.

The work to be done by each visitor, the golden rule, interpreted by a clear head and a warm heart, will always sufficiently suggest. Temporal necessities must first be cared for, since those who are in pain from hunger or neglect are not apt listeners to moral and religious truth. Hunger can be appeased, nakedness covered, and enforced idleness supplied with work; if not from the visitor's own resources, by his application to individuals or organizations, who stand always ready to meet such exigences as soon as they are made known; and there are good physicians who never refuse to respond to a call for the sick poor.

These most pressing wants supplied, the more common duties of Christian friendliness begin : by a stated — yet never impertinent — oversight, to see that the children are washed, clothed, and getting their share of that free instruction which the city munificently gives during the week, and that they find a place in some good Sabbath school upon the Lord's day; to win the confidence and grateful friendship of all, and to make them feel that it is Christ (not the visitor) whom they ought to thank, because all is done for the love and pleasure, and in the service, of Christ; and so, with no rude shock to old prejudice or adverse creed, gradually to make them "believe the works," and then believe in the visitor's religion "for the very work's sake," until, knowing these Church-members by their works, and judging their faith by its fruits, these cleansed and purified households shall be won toward that interest in religion and its ordinances which shall make them Sabbath-keepers and sanctuary attendants; and, by God's blessing, eventually add them to the number of the lost who are found.

The value of such working, Christian friendship as this can scarcely be over-estimated. It revives hope in the minds of those who, by so many discomfitures in their hard battle of life, were getting disheartened as well as weary; it recalls self-respect to breasts from which it had well-nigh for ever flown; it restrains from fresh excesses, by the natural desire to stand well in the eyes of a new and valuable acquaintance; it awakens confidence in the almost abandoned idea, that it may be possible, if not to realize all the bright visions of youth, yet to "do well" in the world still; it sweetens all that sour and rancid misanthropy which had been cankering the spirit, and brings back that sense of kindliness toward humanity which is the first step in the path to confidence in God. And thus, little by little,— sometimes with many pull-backs and wearisome postponements,— it mitigates the harshness of poverty, disinfects the soul of those vices which are so apt to claim poverty for their own, and so prepares the way for Christ to enter into the swept and garnished heart, and then for these prodigal children to find a home in the courts of the Lord.

Happy the Church which can point to groups of its own faithful members, and say, "And such were some of you; but ye are washed, but ye are sanctified, but ye are justified in the name of the Lord Jesus, and by the Spirit of our God"!

And happy the Christian who can feel, that, by the cheap — though sometimes seemingly very dear — assignment of perhaps one afternoon of every week to such always arduous, often repellant, sometimes exceedingly self-denying, yet invariably rewarding labors, he has not only earned his own honest, Christian self-respect, and kept the pulses of spiritual life throbbing with more of the vigor and joy of health in his own breast, and made himself happy in the restored happiness of others; but has been permitted to give aid to the gracious Master in the matter of His great solicitude, "that His banished be not expelled from Him;" and earned the right humbly to hope for that Divine approval at the judgment which will welcome him who has been "faithful over a few things" to the everlasting joy of that

Lord Who will say, "Inasmuch as ye have done it unto one of the least of these My brethren, ye have done it unto Me"!

(7.) It will almost necessarily happen, that that Church which undertakes vigorously to carry on such a home-missionary work as this will soon find it needful to make provision for gathering in the fruits of it, at least in some degree, upon the field itself. It can hardly be long before a mission chapel will be demanded, for the shelter of that mission school which Christian wisdom will suggest, as the best agency for the Sabbath instruction of the little children of the poor. They will be more at their ease there than they would be, if merged in the multitude of the home school of the Church. Local attachments will soon bind them to it as *their* chapel. A style of dress and behavior — very natural, and quite pardonable always, in such a school — will excite no comment there, which might breed a difficulty elsewhere. While, as it is their chapel and their school, and entirely theirs, the whole service can be managed to interest and benefit them in all their peculiarities, as it could not be, if other — and in some sense discordant — claims upon consideration were perpetually crowding themselves upon the thought of its superintendent. There, too, some simple, stated, Sabbath worship, as a kind of apprenticeship to the regular sanctuary service — perhaps, with lay preaching from some missionary of the City Missionary Society, or other competent person — will be very likely soon to be demanded and supplied; which will gather in many of the children of the mission school, with their parents and other adults, who will be willing to assemble there, when they are not yet quite prepared, from considerations of dress, distance, or, it may be, prejudice, to " give thanks in the great congregation," and praise God " among much people." Led gradually along, thus, the time will come when personally accepting Christ as their Saviour, and desiring to own him before men, they will look toward the Church which has through these agencies stretched out its kind, supporting arms to their relief, with a feeling of affectionate gratitude and yearning desire which will instinctively claim membership there, saying, " Where thou lodgest, I will lodge; thy people shall be my people; and thy God, my God."

Thus the Church which wisely uses mission

chapels in connection with its missionary work will find constant re-action of strength from them; while through them, — if distributed among the waste places with that sagacity, and used with that wisdom, which a general plan embracing all may secure, — the entire needy territory of the city may be, at least in some degree, reformed and permeated by a Sabbath-keeping influence.

Great good has already been realized from mission schools and mission chapels; and those evils which are now obvious in connection with them — by which their benefactions of clothing are sometimes ill-applied; by which some localities are overworked by them, the same children attending on the same day two or three different schools, while other places are wholly overlooked by their influence; by which many children are so occasional in their attendance as scarcely to be relied on, except when some special, festive attraction invites — would all be removed; while their efficiency would be indefinitely strengthened, by bringing them out of their present sporadic aspects, and giving each one its symmetrical place in a general plan covering the whole area of the city, and, in a specific one, assigning it as the centre around which circle, and whither tend, the daily home-missionary labors of the working members of some one Christian Church.

(8.) The only remaining suggestion to which space can here be afforded is, that this home-missionary work of every Church should have a recognized position among its public remembrances, counsellings, and prayers, correspondent to that important place which of right it holds among its labors. No undertaking of this description, involving the constant co-operation of so many laborers, can habitually flourish without recurrent revision; and that frequent renewing of popular interest in it, which shall keep crowding upon all who ought to be its participants, a feeling of its import and the gravity of its neglect. The enterprise of foreign missions is one of the greatest works which God has laid upon the conscience of the Church, and none could make clearer or louder appeal to every sanctified nature. Yet experience has shown, that, without the vigorous and skilful use of the "Monthly Concert" to awaken interest in all the details of the labor, and to freshen before the Christian mind the force of those motives of the Gospel which look that way, it would be difficult to maintain that general degree of constant and self-denying desire for its success by which alone its operations can be financially sustained, and its constant calls for laborers met. By parity of reasoning it may be urged, that no Church can reasonably expect to succeed in the endeavor to Christianize thoroughly that territorial "parish," which constitutes its fair share of the general work to be done for Christ in the city, without a similar arrangement of regular review and appeal. The last Sabbath evening of every month has been thus, in some cases, observed as the "Home Concert," with a success which has been sufficient to give assurance of the wisdom of the plan, and to make it safe to refer to it, as essential to the reasonably perfect development of the home-missionary work.

It should be managed so as to unite, at every step, a review of the wants of the field, and an accurate statistical account of what has been done to supply them since the last Concert, with an appeal, on the one hand, to the Christian principle of the Church to supplement what is obviously lacking; and, on the other, to God to add His blessing. A good order of arrangement might be this: Let the superintendent of the home Sabbath-school tell the story of the month in his department. Let the superintendents of the mission schools — for any faithful church which honestly accepts this work must soon have more than one — follow, in their order. Then let the deacon who superintends the systematic visitation of the " parish " give his statistics for the month, including the whole number of subdivisions for which the Church is responsible; the number of such subdivisions (if any) remaining unassigned to any worker; the number of visits reported to him as having actually been made during the month; the number of tracts distributed, of poor children clothed, or gathered to the day, or Sunday, schools, of poor persons helped to employment, &c., &c., with all details and incidents, either of past supply or of present need, which may deepen the sympathy of the Church with the work. Let there be, then, a report of chapel services and of neighborhood prayer-meetings which have been held. Let the officers of the Church follow, with some account of their visits to the sick and the afflicted; and the pastor speak last, with a similar report of his own labor for the month, including the statistics of the Church, the whole number of its present members, the additions since the last report, the losses by dismission and death, adding some obituary notice of members deceased (for surely Church members ought not to be allowed to drop out of the fraternal circle into the grave, with no other "sign" than the mortuary asterisk on the name list), and adding such suggestions as may seem pertinent, by way of correcting any thing amiss, or urging on the faithful toil. Let each previous speaker be followed by some brother, who shall implore the special blessing of the Lord upon that portion of the general service to which the attention of all has just been turned, the pastor closing by prayer, commending the whole work to the Saviour's grace. Let any brother, at any time, interject any earnest thought, which may glance light from his mind upon any dark place. And let every prayer be followed by the impromptu singing of a verse or two of some rousing lyric. Let every report be brief; and let every speaker avoid mere generalities as he would the pestilence.

Such a meeting, as the rule, will be a crowded one, and full of interest. Many will say, "It is the best meeting of the month." It will be the "best," because it will do more than all things, without it, can do to stimulate the people of God to expect great things, and attempt great things, in the desire of making the city of their habitation as "the garden of God."

This, then, is the answer to our question: The *Churches of Christ* must carry the Gospel to the needy and the neglected of Boston. They cannot do it simply by using the ordinary "means of grace." They cannot do it by deputation to the City Missionary, or any other society. They can only do it by making every one of their own members a home missionary, — the very thing which God commands, and Christ expects, and for which the millennium waits; the very thing which the essential principles of Christianity so require, that, to be excused from it, any believer must prove himself an exception to all the common laws of grace.

Let every Church undertake this duty; let it believe that God will make success in the performance of it, not only possible, but sure; in conference with its sister Churches, let it divide with them the area for which all are jointly responsible, and accept its proper share; let it subdivide that share into two or three hundred groups, averaging from five to ten families each; then let it fill those sub-divisions by volunteers from its own number; and let those volunteers enter upon, and patiently pursue, the labor of intelligent, helpful, Christian friendship for the families for which they become responsible; and let the wise patience of that friendship, after brightening their earthly lot, gradually lead its beneficiaries to the mission chapel, the sanctuary, the cross; and let the work be animated and energized at the Home Concert, month by month.

Let the Churches, — at the very least, until they can suggest some plan more impregnated with the wisdom and power of the Gospel, — *attempt* this, and prove God, and see if he will not save the poor and the vile " out of all their dwelling-places wherein they have sinned; and cleanse them, and make them His people, and be their God."

www.ingramcontent.com/pod-product-compliance
Lightning Source LLC
Chambersburg PA
CBHW021213240426
43667CB00038B/363